THE ENGLISH SECRET
AND OTHER ESSAYS

THE
ENGLISH SECRET

AND OTHER ESSAYS

BY

BASIL DE SÉLINCOURT

Essay Index Reprint Series

BOOKS FOR LIBRARIES PRESS, INC.
FREEPORT, NEW YORK

First Published 1923
Reprinted 1968

LIBRARY OF CONGRESS CATALOG CARD NUMBER:

68-16927

NOTE

ALL these essays were written for *The Times Literary Supplement.* I hope its kind Editor, when he sees them in their bulk, will feel no pang. He is responsible for them in more senses than one.; not least in having founded an institution to which those who love the name of England turn constantly for knowledge of the deeper sources of her life.

CONTENTS

I

THE ENGLISH SECRET

THE problem of education is in the forefront of public attention at the present time, and the Government, like the country, has been seriously preoccupied with it. Within the last few years four reports have been issued, devoted in turn to the teaching of the classics, of modern languages, of science, and of English. Each of these reports has been the work of a committee not of mere specialists, but of men who combine special knowledge with a wide outlook on affairs; and yet, broadly considered, the result of their deliberations has been in each case to claim more attention, both relatively and absolutely, for the particular branch of study which they had been asked to examine. The total effect of their labours, therefore, is to convince us, as we were otherwise only too willing to believe, that youth is shorter than it should be. We misquote La Fontaine, and say with a sigh:

> Il nous en faut au moins un siècle bien compté,
> Car vingt ans, ce n'est pas la peine !

The human mind matures too rapidly. We have taken our bias and fallen into a routine, before we have assimilated a hundredth part of the information which we need or learned the use of a quarter of those delicate tools which are the furniture of our intellectual workshop. As the experience of the race widens and the scope of the normal life is enlarged, our children seem doomed to a more and more unenviable lot. With three or four different teachers competing for every hour of their time, it is difficult to see how they are to secure the background of repose which seems to

2747   B

be a condition of all growth and of the mind's most of all. The watched pot never boils. Once we begin to pursue our ideals of education in an atmosphere charged, however little, with excitement and self-consciousness, we shall stifle the very faculties we wish to develop and defeat the ends we have in view, though they be in themselves the highest and the best.

Perhaps, then, it is not wholly a misfortune that, at a time when important developments in the organization of our educational system are looked for, the Government should find itself temporarily deprived of the means of carrying them out. The war overwhelmed us financially; but it did more and worse : our faculty of experience itself was dislodged by it. All the reports on education were written under the impact of the shock. The nation, the Empire, had pulled through, but on a margin of strength with which no one could feel satisfied. The impulse was strong to profit at once from all our bitter lessons of insufficiency and to apply the necessary remedies. We did not know enough about our neighbours, we must all learn French and German ; we were behind-hand in invention and in the chemistry and mechanics of production, it was because science had been inadequately taught ; compared with the Canadian or the New Zealander, we were mere sleep-walkers, we must above all find ourselves and discover what we stood for, we must learn English ; and, of course, the disposition to pursue any of these accomplishments at the expense of the classics must be resisted to the last gasp. Such, expressed in the crudest possible terms, is the upshot of the different advices which have been tendered to a distracted Government. The whole of them are clearly of the nature of good resolutions.

The framers of the report on the teaching of English were deeply impressed by the prominence accorded in the systematized education of France to the national language and literature. They seem to have realized imperfectly how much our problem is complicated in this country by the fact that the people we have to educate is the English people. It is a comparatively easy matter to educate a Frenchman. Not only is he alive from the start, asking for it, tingling with susceptibilities and reverberations; he also finds ready to hand that incomparable instrument, French: a language which has set its house in order and, having understood itself, can make a confident appeal to the intelligence of which it is to be the pattern. How different the nature and the condition of our English children, who, every time we return from beyond the Channel, strike us, beside the shining porcelain of those clear French faces, as so much half-formed, unreflecting clay! They are not consumed with anxiety to learn anything; least of all has it ever crossed their minds that they must learn English. And how shall we teach it to them, when the few of us who have begun to know what it is know it to be a tissue of accommodations, a thing with which order, method, and all that the developing mind first apprehends and rests upon have nothing to do—in a word, a kind of miraculous flowering of man's still unconscious wisdom, preserved to us as a compensation for our many blunderings, as a reward for our patience in confusion and our fundamental faith in life?

It was natural that the war, with its vicissitudes and difficult victory, should be followed by an outbreak of patriotism. No people is, in the last resort, more patriotic than the English, or readier to make ultimate sacrifices for the safety and welfare of their country. Yet our patriotism is normally of the kind which is not exhibited. The tendency which many must have noticed among us in these last years to ' discover ' and to ' push ' English literature or English music, to say nothing of trade or the Empire, and to conjure up a sense of magical virtue which must attach to these things because they are English, is uncharacteristic of our race. England, as good judges know, was once the leading country of the world in music, and there is no reason why she should not regain that position ; but she is likeliest to regain it if she is allowed to retain her natural unconcern about her own performances and to think the works of Smith, Brown, and Robinson as dull as, or even a little duller than, they are. The case of our literature is still more vital. What attitude are we to take towards the strong and growing movement of which Sir Henry Newbolt's report is but one sign—the movement which aims at raising English to a leading place in education and conceives of it as offering in itself all that is necessary to the development of the mind and the ripening of every faculty ?

This movement is, of course, primarily a ' humanistic ' movement : its ostensible aim is to make our education more living and more real ; so far as this is its direction, our sympathy with it is unqualified. But it is tinged also with that narrower, that un-English patriotism ; and so it comes about that the ardent claims it advances in support of an English culture suffer from a defect, the last, we may be sure, their advocates could suspect in them : they are inadequate. The English language, English literature, stand, in our view, for something even greater than the report allows. There was an old dilemma of the schools about the teaching of virtue, a dilemma which arose largely because virtue is unseizable, an influence permeating and proceeding from the whole man, an atmosphere. The quality of the English spirit is similar ; we believe it to be a question of the subtlest and most serious import how far and by what processes it can be taught, if indeed it can be directly taught at all.

Here we must at once make a distinction. The spirit which we identify as essentially English appears in innumerable simplicities of form, which still fall naturally from the lips of any English child. Who does not know the lovely carol refrain ?

> The rising of the sun
> And the running of the deer,
> The playing of the merry organ,
> Sweet singing in the choir.

There is not a village in the land to which its sweetness is not native and congenial. But the constituents of that sweetness, the rhymes that are no rhymes, the ebb and flow of rhythm, the incoherencies of thought, the incompleteness, the audacity, the impressionism, the post-impressionism—how many understand or could hope to understand these things ? Just as the true appreciation of Milton has been said to be the last reward of the scholar, so a finished critical delight in these racial innocencies is given to those alone who have traced the interplay of thought and form in poetry through all its elaborations. We need to have seen where Euripides failed on one side, or Racine on another, before we are qualified to appreciate this anonymous English success.

In so far, then, as the teaching of English means the assurance to English children of an immediate experience of the English spirit as it lives in English letters, or English music, or English life, who can overestimate the importance of this ? It could be done, if the teachers were unsophisticated like their pupils. But the teachers, alas ! must be educated and cannot be more than partially educated men. They know that they must pronounce their *h*'s where others pronounce them and must mind their *p*'s and *q*'s. The glimmerings of method and principle to which they have been introduced at Oxford or at Birmingham have amazed instead of enlightening them ; their native sense of beauty has withered and the love of bathos flourishes in its place. They drape the windows of poetry with Nottingham lace curtains and keep an aspidistra in a pot behind ; and the fault is with English, not with them. For it has none of the qualities that can recommend it to intermediate appreciation. Every Frenchman is a stylist ; the veriest peasant discriminates between accuracy and inaccuracy in the use of words, taking as his model a luminous prose. The corresponding Englishman is unaware of the existence of any model. He reads the Bible, he reads *John Bull*, and believes that the prophet Isaiah and Mr. Bottomley teach the same righteousness in the same manner.

The point is vital, and needs our more scrupulous and wider consideration. The English spirit, we hold, is distinguished in all its manifestations, and not least in its language and literature, by its power to carry forward and preserve under stress qualities which, in one after another of the races that have contributed most to the civilization of the world, we see sacrificed to the attainment of some special function. It is the normal tendency of the mind, as it confronts the impact of experience and steers its way through the adverse current, to submit its faculties to division, to distinguish the different methods which are applicable to different contingencies, and so to furnish itself with certain specific implements or limbs. Now our physical limbs themselves are subject to this grave disadvantage, that having them in one kind we cannot have them in another. The birds when they took to flying sacrificed the use of fingers and hands for ever, to become the beautiful and ineffectual angels we see to-day. The case is infinitely more serious where the development of the mind is at stake. The mind is a mirror, and its most precious attribute is responsiveness. But, as it forms itself to the mould of the world, it tends to warp to-morrow's experience by refractions from the experience of yesterday. The lesson which it has the greatest difficulty in learning is that all specialization of its powers must be conducted under a reserve, and that its life is its faculty to remain, if we may express it so, whole before a world that is whole. The chief exponent of this truth in recent years has been a prominent French philosopher. But the broad tendencies of French civilization are diametrically and dangerously opposed to it. Only the other day, one of the leaders of French criticism, M. René Doumic, summarizing the merit and virtue of Louis XIV and his time, wrote :

Il a humilié la nature devant la raison, en qui réside toute la noblesse de l'homme. Ainsi il a exalté nos énergies traditionnelles et amené à son plein épanouissement l'âme de la race.

The weak spot in French intellectual armour could not be better indicated. No doubt, reason may more nearly claim to represent the wholeness of the mind than any other faculty, especially if we use the word in its most comprehensive significance. But it is not and never can be the whole ; least of all when it looks for its triumphs in the humiliation of nature. The French, then, with all the high specialization and pride of their intellectual consciousness, have divided the mind and, in dividing, limited it. The English, without knowing what they were about, have in a singular degree preserved it whole. Our usual name for this wholeness is simply common sense. Respecting Nature instead of 'humiliating' her, watching facts as they are instead of demonstrating what they must and shall be, we have built up our Constitution, our Empire, and all those astonishing combinations of the theoretically senseless and the practically sane and sound which everywhere go by the name of English. Our conclusion is that this quality of the

English mind, which we call common, has nothing common about it at all; it is a rarity, and it is of priceless value. To it more than to any other power we know belongs the task of guiding the spirit of man through the new phases of his development. We are trustees of the future of the world. Is that future to be brighter or is it to be gloomier than the past? On us more than on any other nation the answer depends, not primarily because of our position or our wealth—in these we are easily outdone,—but because long-rooted experience in the past has matured, without specializing, our power of vision. It is time, then, that we should reflect seriously upon the nature and implications of this remarkable gift, so that we may do nothing to weaken or undermine it. In framing a policy of education, above all, we must go warily; for a chief part of the educational process is the replacement of unconscious by conscious action of the mind, and, broadly speaking, this great English virtue is a virtue of unconsciousness.

It must, so far as the bulk of the nation is concerned, remain a virtue of unconsciousness. The difficulty which we found in the qualification of primary school teachers for the communication of the English spirit through music or letters is, we greatly fear, insuperable. We are not of those who hold that great art explains itself or that its appeal has an emotional universality like that of religion. Least of all do we find such a quality of aesthetic translucence in English master-pieces. Most of those who love our country and our literature must continue to love them without knowing why, and will risk their love itself if they insist on inquiring into the reason of it. But in minds susceptible of the highest and largest development the unconsciousness we speak of has, of course, never been more than partial, and the conditions of the time are less favourable to it every day. As life goes on the world offers our race less scope for the more obvious expression of its abilities. We shall expand less in the future, if only because there is no room for quick expansion now ; and, since our development is to be internal, we must learn to look within. Even if there were no practical motive, our national age, our five hundred years of literary history, compel us to such a course. We cannot any longer ignore what we signify. We have to establish a system of English culture which can maintain as conscious virtue that loyalty to known truth, that simple receptiveness when the new fact appears, that attitude of reserve, that modesty in face of the unknown, that submission of logic to experience, which are now instinctive in us.

To put it otherwise, we have to decide what *learning English* really means. It is a problem in two parts. What is it to learn language ? what is it to learn the English language ? We are far too apt to suppose that language is the whole of education. It is, of course, more potent in its appeal than any other branch of study, and the highest developments are unattainable except by means of it. But, as an educational instrument, it has the disadvantage of appealing entirely to secondary and transposed experiences. It presents no tangible picture, it evokes no immediate response. It is liable, therefore, either to lead nowhere, in the case of minds to which its mutations do not occur readily, or, in the case of minds peculiarly apt to them, to lead into a world little related to our common experience—into an unreal world, in short. We are often disappointed that so few of those who pass through the educational mill learn to appreciate literature, to understand the best uses to which language can be put ; but have we good reason for surprise ? The experience of literature is one in which easier and more elementary experiences are implied, and in these easier experiences we offer the developing mind no practice. So far as we are aware, it is not recognized in English secondary education that the portals of experience are the eye and the ear : and that for the development and refinement of these senses, the gateways through which all wisdom must pass, there is in each case an art, an art ancillary to literature, and at once easier and more obviously educational because of its more direct appeal to instinctive physical responses. Music and the plastic arts, the one more abstract, the other more concrete than literature, are admirably qualified to bring out its central and inclusive place and to exhibit by contrast its delicate equilibrium. Music, particularly, in some respects the most elusive of the arts, furnishes the quickest approach to the conscious appreciation of all artistic effect ; for while its mechanics are of mathematical simplicity and beauty (and an ideal educational instrument on that account), their meaning and value appear only when they are practically applied : they require us to take our part in various easy activities in which an artistic quality makes itself felt from the first. It is almost ludicrous to reflect that among the picked thousand of English men and women who year by year base their culture upon an Hellenic inspiration not a tithe are acquainted with the relations of the musical scale which, in its still imperfect form, had already been seen by the Greeks to be the meeting ground of the arts and the sciences, more essential than the alphabet, and not less elementary. We cannot pursue this topic ; if we have insisted on the value of the elements of music in education, what might we not also say of the urgent demand in England for the better training of the eye, when already our whole civilization is menaced by the unheeded degradation of its visible expression ? Here is a subject which would take us much too far. Our suggestion that music and the plastic arts are ancillary

to literature has been made less in any hope of an early
modification of our higher education to include them
—though indeed there are already some signs of
coming change—than as a means to the clearer pre-
sentment of the position of English literature as we
conceive it.

For English, in our view, stands to other literatures
in a relation analogous to that which we have given
to literature itself among the arts. The stuff of music
is the directly audible sound, of painting the visible
forms of the world, and the scope of each of these arts
is limited and clarified by its immediate appeal to
sense. The stuff of literature involves a transcending
of sense experience ; for the shape and sound of words
do not explain their meaning. To read is to be lifted
by the power of a symbolic code into an ideal region ;
and in no art is the transition so difficult as in literature
between the means and the end. The effects of poetry
are not modelled upon primary appearances, or confined to any single attribute of things ; its inspiration
comes from a vision of concealed significances, its
theme is the developing life of man. Now the English
mind, as we have seen, has a native affinity for
unanalysed adjustments and reactions. Here lies the
secret of the greatness of our literature, here also the
secret of its elusiveness. It comprehends better than
any other the conditions and the opportunities of
literary expression. To understand it is about as
easy and about as difficult as to understand life itself.
Possessed of the ultimate and essential gift, clinging
in defiance of ridicule and the demands of consistency
to their intuition of the relevant fact, the English, in
their literature as elsewhere, disregard the appearances
and superficialities of reason and method and retain,
as by a miracle, just those elements which are vital to
the work in hand. There is only one way of learning
the secret of this extraordinary process : it is to learn

everything else. The study of English literature is a study in compromise, in intuition ; and the method of it is the study of the influences between which compromise has been made. The civilization our literature reflects is a complex of many civilizations that have preceded it, the Greek and Roman above all ; to know the world we live in presupposes knowledge of those precedent worlds. This, to our minds, is the unanswerable case for classical studies. English is unknowable without them. They are the road, and the only road, to conscious appreciation of our own thought and our own times.

A last word touching the relation of French and English culture. After the classics, no study is of greater importance for us than that of the language and literature of France. The breadth of purpose which distinguishes our literature has involved it in only too many technical uncertainties ; one of the chief dangers attaching to the direct study of English, to English conceived as an instrument rather than as the end of education, is that it provides no safeguard against confusion between the virtue of breadth and the vice of uncertainty or bungling. French writers exhibit to us in an eminent degree the beauties of precision. Exquisite marksmen, they give us as we read them the delight of clearly distinguishing the rings of the target and of registering the impeccable shots. It is an experience of the greatest value for us. But again it is an experience fraught with dangers, and to these dangers only too many Englishmen succumb. France claims to be the Attica of modern Europe, and those to whom the literature of Athens is unfamiliar accede to the claim and suppose that the functions of literature, the life from which it receives and to which it gives inspiration, are better understood by our neighbours than by ourselves. If our conception is the true one, that idea is wholly illusory.

English poetry, with all its failings, represents the Greek spirit expanded and, if partly clouded in the process, reinforced. French poetry is quintessential, a refinement of the refined ; a model of method, it is comparatively insignificant in substance, because it has sacrificed truth to perfection and to reason life.

But the message of English literature, of the English spirit, is the culmination of all that the world has yet to offer to the inquiring mind. We cannot effectively receive it unless we are familiar with the elements it holds in solution, the pitfalls it has avoided, the experiences it has incorporated, and unless, when all these things are analysed and appreciated, we still hold fast to the organic principle of the whole, to its prevailing creative integrity. Moreover, the sense of our primary position can only be a misfortune to us unless it goes with a clear recognition of every inadequacy and error. Too much of our English criticism is insular, consisting in the admiration of incidental faults in what is great or of the meanderings of authors who have lost their way. Our poetry, still more our prose, has grown in a soil where weed and seed sprout with equal vigour, and it will be lamentable, it will be fatal, if the love of what is English should mean that we love both alike. English, let us remember it, offers us no standards of discrimination ; that is the price it has to pay for its subtlety and comprehensiveness. The Englishman who is to enter perfectly into his inheritance must be a citizen of the world.

September 1922.

II

A FRENCH ROMANTIC

In one of Lamartine's very early letters, letters
which date from his period of ' immersion dans une
jeunesse légère et corrompue ', when his philosophy of
life fluctuated with the whims of the divinity of the
moment, becoming very gloomy when she became
indifferent, we find him writing to a friend :

What a terrible darkness surrounds us ! How happy are
those careless beings who make a show of sleeping through it
all ! It is easy enough to reject systems as I have done, but
to construct others or to find foundations is a different matter.
I seem to see clearly enough what cannot be, but why does
Heaven so carefully veil from us what is ? Or anyhow, since
it is ordained we should be ignorant eternally, why this insati-
able curiosity that devours us ?

Lamartine shortly afterwards regulated his life by
arranging a marriage with an English girl whose hand
he obtained by affecting to love her ; but he never
quite smoothed out his pleated brain or overcame the
tendency to exalt or abase the gods according to the
state of his digestion. ' Pourquoi le ciel nous voile-t-il
si bien ce qui est ? ' The outcry is absurd on the lips
of a spoiled baby, and Lamartine when he made it
was little more. But there is one point of sense and
candour in it, its admission that much truth is hidden
from us. And if Lamartine floundered in romanticism long after unruly youth could justify him, the
reason was not only in his egotism and sentimentality ;
it was partly that the sense of the mystery of things
remained with him, that the striving for the ideal was
never wholly extinguished in his mind, and that he
was loyal to the idea of truth.

We are not to-day occupied with Lamartine, but with M. Charles Maurras. A gulf yawns between the two men, and yet there is one point of resemblance between them which is significant. M. Maurras's introduction to literary activities was an immersion similar to Lamartine's, the difference being that when the time came for emergence he chose the other side of the pool. While in it he disported himself, we should imagine, quite as energetically as his great predecessor. His riotous individualism led him at one time so far even as to deny the validity of mathematics. However, he emerged; and he emerged with an utter hatred of romanticism stamped upon his very soul. He had divined that the one essential for life was order; he was prepared to worship order wherever he found it and, with one exception, at whatever cost. The exception is a curious one. The conduct of the individual, says M. Maurras, is no one's affair but his own. ' Nous ne sommes pas des gens moraux ! ' Order is not to proceed from within but to be applied from without. It is our solemn duty to impose it upon the world. We have not to convince but to subdue the individual. It is not necessary, therefore, that ideas should be just, provided that they sufficiently seem so; what is necessary is that they should be trenchant and operative. Truth sinks into the second place, and the law of life is expediency.

To the English mind, with its traditional experience of order as the fruit of character and independence, such an attitude verges on the incomprehensible ; and it is for the sake of ranging M. Maurras in some kind of intelligible relation that we have advanced our shocking comparison of this apostle of reason and measure with Lamartine. It is possible, we would suggest, to hate romanticism romantically. Romanticism is an excess of emotion ; and the emotion is not necessarily of the expressive, it may be of the restrictive, kind. The excess may be not of love, but of fear. In general, romanticism is to be distinguished from classicism by its attitude to the fundamental mystery of life, the element of infinity. The achievement of classicism is to accept and place that element, to acknowledge it without denying reason. No art can truly be called classical that is not entire. The tendency of romanticism is to be preoccupied and haunted by the sense of the infinite; and the preoccupation takes two forms. We have the natural romantics, like Lamartine, who variously weep and rave; and we have the unnatural romantics, like M. Maurras, who attempt to exorcize the demon, or believe, as Christian Scientists do, that the evil thing will disappear if they continue to disregard it long enough. For M. Maurras the infinite is the chaotic, and his gospel of order is based upon his horror of chaos. Having experienced chaos in his own person, he concludes that the impulses of men have no intrinsic reasonableness and can only be *rangés* by the operation of some foreign authority and control. Reason is a social not an individual possession, and truth is a kind of social discovery, society's chief task being to mould the individual into conformity with it.

That M. Maurras's orderliness is of a romantic turn we infer, first, from the inconsistencies through which it leads him. He holds, for example, that civilization's nearest approach to perfection in modern times is the Catholic Church. But the centre and motive of Catholicism being belief in God, M. Maurras cannot bring himself to share that belief. What he so fervently admires in Catholicism is its organization, its principles of training: that it has solved all our difficulties, offers us the ready-constructed system lack of which was so painful to Lamartine, and can teach the young adventuring spirit not only what to think but how to arrive at thinking it. The discipline has

partially failed where M. Maurras himself is concerned ;
yet we must observe that it is not, from his point of
view, a weakness in Catholicism that it should confess
a God in a Godless world ; that so vast an organization
should have maintained itself for centuries on the
void is, to him, but additional evidence of its political
and social virtue. For he regards it as the essential
achievement of civilized life to bring order out of
elements that have in themselves no principle of
order, and to found beauty on chaos. Then the Roman
Catholic system, though not itself hereditary, has
always agreed well with the principle of hereditary
authority, of paternal government, in the affairs of
this world. Even in France most Catholics love the
idea of monarchy, and M. Maurras has dedicated his
life to the restoration of the French Royal House. But
he is quite innocent of disruptive intentions, and,
betraying here again his romanticism, conceives of his
policy as one of continuity and fulfilment.

The ideas of M. Maurras are, it may appear, almost
too extreme to merit serious consideration ; they
cannot but arrest our attention when we remember
how great their influence is. M. Maurras is the chief
moving spirit of a strong and united party, prepared,
if occasion should arise, to translate his words into
deeds. It is the quality of effectiveness in his writing
which seems to have determined M. Thibaudet's
treatment in the volume he has recently brought
out.[1] M. Albert Thibaudet, who is a regular con-
tributor to the *Nouvelle Revue Française*, has special
claims on English sympathy, because of his extensive
and discriminating studies of our thought and literature. He has lately written on George Eliot, Defoe,
Herbert Spencer, bringing to the consideration of
each a charming freshness, never content merely to

---

[1] ' Les Idées de Charles Maurras ', par Albert Thibaudet. (Éditions
de la *Nouvelle Revue Française*. 7 f. 50.)

repeat or modify an accepted interpretation. Perhaps
no English author more sadly needed to be seen anew
by our great neighbours than did Herbert Spencer.
M. Thibaudet certainly deserves well of us. But, of
course, his chief concern is with his own country. He
has been occupied during the last few years, in the
intervals of military service, with one of those large
gestes of national self-consciousness which are the
natural culmination of critical activity in France. His
work is announced in the form of a tetralogy, bearing
the general title *Thirty Years of French Life*. The
period of which he treats runs from 1890 to 1920,
years which ' form ', he says, ' for reasons which will
be made clear in the concluding volume, a *mortalis
aevi spatium*, a generation's tableland, as clearly
limited and defined as the indivisible continuity of
time admits '. Bergson, Barrès, and Maurras have been
responsible, he thinks, for the chief currents of living
influence observable during these thirty years ; and
he takes each in turn as the subject of a monograph,
' The Ideas of Charles Maurras ', ' The Life of Maurice
Barrès ', ' Bergsonisme ' ; then in the last, which is
to be called ' A Generation ', the three chief currents
of influence will be related to all the other influences
which have crossed and mingled with them, and which,
concentrating their puissant and vital splendour on great ideas
as France conceives them, on those original themes that are
as mothers to a nation, made up this solid block, well fashioned
by the hand of fate, these thirty years which have the clear
composition of a landscape.

In Heaven, assuredly, life is the fulfilment of the
idea ; and the more we think the more we see that
it should be so here on earth. But we know that in
England it is not so, and we surmise that in France it
is very much less so than French critics would have
us believe. There is an element of illusion, we fancy,
in every effort to bring the conduct of large masses of

men into close relation with the doctrines of their contemporaries. Even where a people is, as the French are, peculiarly receptive and peculiarly intelligent, the leavening of the lump is a slow process. M. Thibaudet is too good a Bergsonian not to be aware of this, and he is on his guard—but insufficiently.

To return to M. Maurras : the key to his influence is that he is first and last a nationalist. The love of France, even if it takes romantic and perverted forms, has an irresistible appeal for every Frenchman ; so M. Maurras may attack even the Republic, since his theme is that if it were not for her republicanism France would be the first nation of the world, and that in spite of it she is still virtually the first. The average French citizen is even less disposed to be satisfied with his government than we are with ours ; and the insurgent herald of home truths is dear to him, as a Leo Maxse can be dear, for the mere fervour of his devotions. To M. Thibaudet and the intellectuals a second allurement is added in the completeness of the mechanism of M. Maurras's thought ; they are charmed by the philosophical rotundity of its design, and they recognize in this intellectual finish an essentially French trait.

An Englishman might be forgiven for expecting an advocate of monarchy to derive some support for his case from the not wholly despicable example of our own country. England, however, has the misfortune to be situated to the north of France

Sur les humides bords du royaume du vent ;

and M. Maurras is from Provence. From the fact that England and France were for centuries one country his traditionalism has nothing to infer. In the first place, all that is not Latin is in M. Maurras's view more or less barbarous, and that which succeeds among barbarians succeeds for the wrong reasons : you cannot argue from the life of the savage to

the life of the civilized being; in the second place,
English history is the history of the long struggle
of a people with its kings, and what after all is the
English Royal House? What continuity has it had?
Muddles, makeshifts, compromises distinguish its
career, and in that at least it is typically English. In
short, England can show nothing comparable to the
slowly maturing power and wisdom of the House of
Capet. The French king that is to come must come
with the inevitability of a mathematical deduction,
he must be, he is, a clear and demonstrable necessity.
M. Maurras proves it all, proves him, and only leaves
it to the event to produce him.

M. Maurras's case is really an absorbing one ; how,
we ask, can so much ability, so much penetration, so
profound a passion for reason and clarity culminate
in such an extreme wrong-headedness ? M. Thibaudet
does not greatly help us, because he is himself too much
impressed. For English readers his book only serves
to throw new complications around a subject already
in itself too complicated. His covert ironies, his
occasional courteous smile, are powerful but elusive
weapons. To our northern crudeness M. Maurras is
as one butting his head against a wall, and we want
to know why in France, of all countries, an action that
seems so unreasonable is so widely applauded. To
M. Thibaudet it is an accident of M. Maurras's thought
that it is unpractical ; the idea of unity under a king,
of kingship as affording for France the summary of her
past greatness, he regards as a solid acquisition for
French minds, not really affected in its value by the
trifling error which has led M. Maurras to suppose that
her greatness must be summarized in the same way
in the future. To English thinking a practical error
of this kind in a writer whose end and aim is practical
cannot seem trifling. How, then, are we to explain
M. Maurras and how are we to explain his popularity ?

To our apprehension M. Maurras is popular because the error he is committing is one to which the French mind, with all its luminousness, is prone. We have called M. Maurras a romantic ; do we mean, therefore, to suggest that the French are a romantical nation ? We are not afraid even of this paradox. The history of French art undermines the distinction between the romantic and the classical, as we ordinarily understand it. France has lately acclaimed Joan of Arc as her national heroine. The period of classical production in France was, we believe, a great romantic period, the period of which Joan was a retarded flower, the period which saw the building and decorating of the great cathedrals ; and the period was classical in this sense, that the whole energy of the people was concentrated upon the expression of a spiritual interpretation of life. Faith was both the inspiration and the atmosphere ; and though faith, religious faith at any rate, is not a necessary element in that integrity of soul which is the foundation of classical expression, no state of mind more naturally conduces to such integrity ; indeed that ' seeing life whole ', which implies being whole oneself in order so to see it, is all but describable as a state of faith. However, the faith of mediaeval France was specifically religious as well as universally engrossing ; and the forms of art which resulted had in consequence that intrinsic determination without which art is never fully itself, is never classical. The French cathedrals mirror the whole life of mediaeval Europe, and so great was the fervour of devotion engaged in their conception and execution that the bearer of a spark, St. Francis, took the conflagration into his own country and produced there, too, a ferment which took shape at last in the *Divina Commedia*. The French had no mediaeval literary classic ; their language was not ready for this culminating expression

of thought and faith ; but the fire of inspiration, the
overflowing joy in life which made it possible were
of French origin. By the time the French language
emerges as an artistic vehicle, the blue skies have
suffused themselves with a veil of grey ; it is the era
of inquiry, whose motto is *Que sçais-je ?* and thence-
forward the genius of the nation is analytical. So
imperious is the impulse to define, divide, and qualify,
that the realm of poetry itself is invaded and laid
under subjection ; and we have at last the phenomenon
of a people, acknowledged to be arbiters of taste, whose
niceness has deprived them of the means of expressing
their whole humanity, and who are so complacent in
their loss as still to teach in their schools and to hold
up for an enduring model of the spirit of their race in
its perfection and purity the works of a period of
formalism.

French poetry, it would seem, has been predomi-
nantly formal because the language crystallized at
a time when excessive scepticism had supervened upon
a too undiscriminating faith. And, alas ! the same
scepticism infected faithful and unfaithful alike, and
decreed that those who chose faith must disavow
freedom. So the wedge was driven deep between two
faculties that require each other. Poetry could not
span that cleavage. Great poetry demands an atmosphere in which circumstance and convention raise
no veil between man and his destiny ; it must confront him immediately with the powers and mysteries
which overarch his life. Shakespeare does this, chaoti-
cally, in an attitude of acknowledged scepticism ;
Corneille and Racine, with their Court vocabulary and
their Hellenic unities, betray the scepticism they do
not acknowledge, and the seeming classical elements
of their drama are, in fact, indications of their self-
distrust. In spite of its exquisitely proportioned
orderliness, their work is in this sense truly romantic,

that the essence of romanticism is inadequacy propping itself upon exaggerations. And the exaggeration in their case is of the same kind as in the case of M. Maurras, it is an exaggeration of fear. Fearful lest they should exceed, they prop themselves excessively.

As an indication of the restrictive severity of the long reign of formalism in French poetry we might quote certain excesses of the natural romantics in their various efforts to free themselves. Few of these efforts, however, have been very consistent or persevering where form is concerned. It seems that the language itself and the great traditions of precision and clarity which have shaped the turn of every phrase impose upon French poetry limitations not inherent in the nature of poetry itself. We prefer to quote a passage of contemporary work, a passage which is doubtless censured for daring antinomianism by French connoisseurs, but which to us seems merely natural. These beautiful lines will have the further advantage of being as yet unfamiliar to many of our readers :

De nouveau après tant de sombres jours le soleil délicieux
  Brille dans le ciel bleu.
L'hiver bientôt va finir, bientôt le printemps commence, et
    le matin
  S'avance dans sa robe de lin.
Après le corbeau affreux et le sifflement de la bise gémissante
  J'entends le merle qui chante !
Sur le platane tout à l'heure j'ai vu sortir de son trou
  Un insecte lent et mou.
Tout s'illumine, tout s'échauffe, tout s'ouvre, tout se dégage,
  Peu à peu croit et se propage
Une espèce de joie pure et simple, une espèce de sérénité,
  La foi dans le futur été !
Ce souffle encore incertain dont je sens ma joue caressée
  C'est la France, je le sais !

We well remember how, as we read them for the first

time, a comparison established itself in our minds immediately with that late-born wonder of Latin poetry which, echoing like a voice from the tomb, seems yet the herald of some distant reawakening, an anticipation of that world of sunshine, birds, and flowers familiarly haunted by every modern poet :

> Ver novum : ver iam canorum ; vere natus orbis est !
> vere concordant amores, vere nubunt alites
> et nemus comam resolvit de maritis imbribus.

The author of the *Pervigilium Veneris* is as one who breaks fetters and casts off a spell ; and, if we are not misled, something of the same sense of an almost magical liberation breathes in Paul Claudel's lines. But whereas in the Latin words we feel that a power alien to their spirit has possessed itself of them and that their measure has been exceeded, in the French we feel that things long forgotten have been remembered and stiffened limbs relaxed. A lovely Psyche, self-immured, has emerged from its prison to float in the light upon its exquisite, translucent wings :

> C'est la France, je le sais !

and the wonder is not that it floats there now, but that it has not always so floated, that it has ever done anything else.

The true France, the France of the crusades and the cathedrals, the France of Ste. Jeanne d'Arc, still lives ; and we can understand with what ardour a Frenchman of to-day, fired with the great traditions of his country, aware that she can never rise to the full measure of her greatness while she is inwardly at strife, must pursue the sacred task of restoring her to unity. That cannot blind our eyes to certain general facts of our time, certain predisposing conditions which must be fulfilled, in France as with us, if men are to agree together. We had in England in the latter half of the last century a great thinker, a great idealist, a great romantic, who made the fundamental error of attempting to impose upon us a system of thought and conduct which assumed machinery to be an abomination. His influence was immense, but it did not deflect by a hair's breadth the overwhelming onward march of industrialism. Machinery is, in the last analysis, one of the forms of knowledge ; and to rebel against knowledge is to rebel against the rising tide. The influence of Ruskin, immense as it still is, might have been immensely greater had he recognized that the ideal itself is conditioned by the epoch. M. Maurras, who is in no way comparable to Ruskin in stature, being no more than a publicist of exceptional energy and accomplishment, commits the same error in a different, a more serious way. Machinery is, after all, external to us. A great nation has lately banished alcohol ; it is conceivable that it may one day banish electricity or steam. These are exterior weapons over which we have an appearance of choice, to take or leave them. Within us, the tool by which we touch all others, is the mind. The workings of the mind are conditioned by the ideas with which it is familiar ; and if a man will never willingly renounce a power of which he has once felt the use, much less will he ever permit a truth once perceived to be veiled from him. The truth may be dangerous, it may be inapplicable to his case, it may be subversive of society ; but if he has seen it, if it has gone abroad, only one course is open to the wise guardians of human destiny. New principles of organization must be found in which the truth in question is fully recognized and in which this very fullness of recognition itself makes possible the safeguards and limitations required for the preservation of the organism. This is what M. Maurras has not perceived ; he would still work with the old categories, still hopes to see contemporary France

accept that strait-jacket which in the comparatively
unenlightened eighteenth century she so violently
split asunder and threw off. His horror of the Revolution (' la Révolution dite Française ', as he says) knows
no bounds ; and yet, from one point of view, the
Revolutionaries were but guilty of the same fault as
his, the fault of pursuing ideas to romantic excesses,
while, from another point of view, they had this merit,
that the ideas they exaggerated were inevitable ideas.

Nothing is easier than to rail at the errors of
modernity, to make mock of the pathetic illusions to
which the chaos of its conflicting aspirations gives
rise. The air is so thick with good intentions that
advocates of ' realization ' are almost to be envied
for the gay time they have pricking the pretty bubbles.
M. Maurras does it with equal grace and firmness—
out of his balloon, which he mistakes for *terra firma*,
while lighter and more vulnerable craft sail by. For
he is no true realist, he is a restrictionist ; and his love
of the classical is the love of an achievement, not of
the achieving power. We suggest that there can be
only one true realism, as there can be only one true,
one classical art, and that the test in both is intellectual
and emotional integrity. We cannot be content,
any more than M. Maurras can, with a life that will
not at the last so organize itself as to be capable of
feeling and expressing a spiritual purpose. We do
not care less for measure and harmony than he does.
But we recognize that measure and harmony are
simply modes of being and that the task for our time
is to achieve, not any order, but our own. That
order alone can satisfy us, that order alone is, therefore,
practicable for us, in which our own nature is fully
expressed ; in which all the fermenting elements of
the modern world, after free expansion and development, shall have taken their true reciprocal relations ;
when we shall be so far masters of our new knowledge

and our new weapons as to bring them to the service of an intelligible end and to see them as functions of one life, a life not only intelligible but also beautiful, a life identified for us in its aim and in the best of its achievement with all those perfect forms which, from the earth under our feet to the sun above us, perpetually rebuke our blunderings and incite us to new worship and to new endeavour. To every age its own problems. We cannot again be classical on the old terms, we cannot be classical again until all our illusions, whether of belief or disbelief, have ripened in a conciliating experience. The goal we work towards is that larger integration. New knowledge has imposed a new constitution upon the life of mankind. We have to create that constitution, to live that life.

September 1920.

III

THE CHALLENGE TO POETRY

ONE of the most significant of modern developments, and one which nevertheless belongs to the more or less unobserved background of our lives, is that of public music. Music is not nearly so familiar a possession of the people as we should like it to be, but it has a greater diffusion than it ever had before, and is capable of a diffusion till now quite unimaginable. The first Handel Festival was held at the Crystal Palace in 1859, Bach's Matthew Passion was first performed in Westminster Abbey in 1871, and all the great choirs which flourish now in different parts of the country, with much of the music they sing, are a product of the intervening years. The love of music is spreading among us, and there is a growing desire, recognized in the Ministry of Education itself, to foster its civilizing influences. A sense of national pride enlists as followers to this movement some minds that might else hold aloof from it. The wealth of English Tudor music has lately been made available to the public. It is beginning to be generally believed that England, having a great past in music, is entitled to hope for a great future.

But the art of music is not only more popular, it is also more appealing, than it ever was before. What wonderful strides it has made as an emotional language since the days of Byrd and Tallis ! In England's musical prime the human voice was still the most important instrument of musical expression, and the relation of music to poetry was close. Its complete independence is now firmly established in the popular mind, and there is as much need to explain the unity as to exhibit the differences between these sister arts. In little more than two centuries there has grown up, one might almost say, a new universe—a universe in which the emotions of men, instead of being removed and subdued by their artistic translation, are heightened and magnified immeasurably. When a man leaves a bridge party or a circle of gay talk before the fire and, walking out into the night, sees the stars in their eternal watch, alien and immutable, he experiences a sense of suspended life, of annihilation in awe before their remoteness ; the heart stops beating, the breath catches, the whole being readjusts itself : how utterly insignificant, after all, are its transitory interests and choices ! But there is similar suspension, a similar catch in the breath, when, in a modern concert room, the transcendent glories of the symphony announce not their remoteness but their nearness to us. These unfathomable intensities of significance, these majestic finalities of decision, are mine ; this splendour, this beauty, is a part of me ; it is man speaking to man. The fountain source of all was, of course, Bach. When Bach had shown the way, there was a surge and uprush of pure music in Central Europe to which nothing in the history of other arts can be compared, unless it be the building of the French cathedrals. It was as if a vast gold-mine had been discovered, opening out to those happy mortals who had first right of entry long galleries of metal, precious and pure ; nor did they waste their matchless opportunity, but tirelessly worked on, minting in streams a beautiful clear coinage which was good in all the markets of the world. Of almost all the great composers of the nineteenth century fertility is the conspicuous trait ; they were limited only by the capacity of their hands to write down what their invention dictated. And what they dictated was, broadly speaking, all good. Haydn's symphonies, Schubert's songs, remain. Countless, they still have meaning for us—more meaning than most of the music of the day. The world had not changed, but the human mind had suddenly found means to appreciate it newly, and the whole story of creation, all the sumptuous diversities of human life, all the accumulated experience of the ages, was virgin soil, a child's garden, of richness and freshness inexhaustible.

However, it is not with the almost riotous exuberance of the classical composers that we are now concerned, but with the condition of the modern ear, now that this great orgy of sound is being poured into it. Here is music, not so new, certainly, as the cinema, but a not less abiding portent, and bound, like the cinema, to capture the attention of the people more and more. What is likely to be the effect of it upon them, and what relation must we expect to see between the reading and the listening public, between the public to which literature and the public to which music is addressed? It is absurd to suppose—yet we believe that a majority of literary critics do suppose —that this rich universe, this other Eden, this demi-Paradise, can have come into being and offer to the multitude its exquisite and attainable fruits, and that those who walk in the garden and taste of them will come forth unaffected, ready to devote the same care and the same attention as once they did to the common plants in their borders. There is undoubtedly a sense in which music is dangerous to poetry—dangerous because its vitality is obvious, while that of poetry is concealed; dangerous because it assaults its hearers and seizes upon them, while poetry patiently awaits her hour. These dangers can only be met, if they can be met at all, by recognition : we must learn to appreciate more clearly what field of excellence belongs to each of the two, what kind of pleasure each best affords, as only so can we avoid injurious and irrelevant comparisons.

How different the basis for comparisons has lately become we may recognize anew and from a fresh

angle if we consider how the poet Shelley was circum-
stanced, and what his musical experience is likely to
have been. At the end of the eighteenth century the
fire of music in England was burned out. In Pepys's
time it had still been one of the natural enjoyments
of a gentleman to take his part in a madrigal; in
Shelley's days new fashions in music were abroad, and
England was one of the last countries in which they
were acclimatized. Handel, it is true, spent most of
his life in England, but he was an appanage of a foreign
Court; Purcell had done great things, but had not
achieved popularity. In any case, few of the facilities
for hearing music which we now enjoy existed for
Shelley, and we may surmise that his principal experience of it was had in Eton College chapel. He had
probably heard the name of Bach and of his own
contemporary Beethoven. Mozart had lived, he had
listened to several of his operas; Schumann and
Chopin had still to be. What, can we suppose, would
the influence of Chopin have been on Shelley's poetry,
had he intimately known his music, as everybody
knows it now? We can hardly ask the question without
perceiving how largely Shelley's work is characterized
by an unconscious rivalry with music, by an aspiration
after forms of expression which the poet divines, but
which elude and tantalize him. Matthew Arnold
long ago said that in his view music would have been
the right sphere for Shelley's genius : had he observed
how frequent in his work is the acknowledgement
that he has touched the limit of verbal expression?
When Shelley's vision rises to ecstasy he 'faints and
fails'; words and the material attachments they
involve lose their value for him. He describes in his
'Hymn to Intellectual Beauty' how his first conception of beauty as an ideal put him beside himself and
deprived him of speech.

Sudden, thy shadow fell on me;
I shrieked, and clasped my hands in ecstasy!

Long years of devotion still left him associating the
spirit of beauty with influences to which language has
no key. Never, he tells us,

> joy illumed my brow
> Unlinked with hope that thou would'st free
> This world from its dark slavery,
> That thou—O awful Loveliness—
> Would'st give *whate'er these words cannot express.*

The poet might perhaps be defined, in this connexion,
as the man whose ecstasies are verbal, and it would be
superfluous to insist how very abundantly Shelley's
were so. It is not the less true that they frequently
carried him to a height, launched him upon a sea, of
emotion to which he felt language inadequate and
irrelevant. He lifts words with him as he climbs,
but they drop away before he is at the summit. He
draws them after him into the surging currents, but
the surge itself sweeps them from his grasp. We seem
indeed in Shelley to have a case of poetry 'aspiring
after the condition of music', and the aspiration, largely
a result of inexperience, is a source of weakness in his
work. He knew enough of music to have felt its
possibilities and to be haunted by them, but for him
these possibilities were all unrealized. Of music as the
expression of the fine, the tense, the tumultuous
vibrations of feeling which were his life he had no
knowledge—he had but a surmise. That the great
empire of love was to be divided, that music was to
annex all its more romantic and mountainous territories,
could not have occurred to him.

This could not have occurred to Shelley, but it is
what has actually happened for all of us; we bow
before the *fait accompli*, and knowing Shelley and
Chopin, Milton and Handel, Beethoven and Shakespeare, we ought, it would seem, to compare more
frequently the experiences they severally afford us,
and, in particular, to inquire what has been and what

is to be the effect on poetry—poetry as it lives in us—
of this new effulgence beside her of the hitherto
submissive, dark, companion star. But there are many
difficulties. Comparisons are the critic's business,
and the critic is a literary man, using words and
inclined to deify them. When he writes about literature he has a comparatively simple task : he has but
to appeal, at his more modest elevation, to the same
faculties as those to which the creative artist appeals
at their heights. But when he writes about music
he is like a philosopher experimenting in relativity ;
all his old standards of measurement measure nothing
in this strange world ; it is as if he had been transported
to those marvellous and distant places, of which the
existence was surmised by Mill, where straight lines
bend and parallels converge. And then the elusiveness of music, its rebellion against the empire of words,
has, we must admit, tilted the balance of criticism
against it. Poetry is the word made magical, and the
critic the man who having felt this magic would have
others feel it. A great part of his energy goes to the
task of communicating to the world his sense of the
charm of poetry, and his absorption is so great that
he is apt to overload or misdirect his praise. The
charms of poetry have indeed been so dispropor-
tionately harped upon that the pages of the poets
suffer ; we have been taught to expect so much from
them that it is not impossible to turn to them and
find them dull. Perhaps the truth may be, that the
quality which the criticism of the time would regard
as essential to poetry—a kind of transfiguration produced in us by sensuous beauty—is not, in fact,
naturally attainable by it except as a sort of superadded
grace, a condescension from heaven ; whereas in music
this quality is natural. No one equally conversant
with poetry and music and wishing to be entranced
could hesitate for a moment to which art to commit

himself. Take any piece of poetry, the most entrancing
you can name—take 'Kubla Khan', or 'La Belle
Dame sans Merci', or 'The Hymn of Pan'—and
compare it for magic with one of Chopin's im-
promptus : the difference is that of a magic I acknowledge, a magic before which I bow down, and a magic
which flows around me, flows into me, saturates me,
lifts me into itself and bears me away on its triumphant
tide. The difference is evident wherever music and
poetry are compared, and it makes the comparison
odious to lovers of poetry.

But—and this is a point we have specially in view—
the comparison is made, in the conditions of modern
life, with ever-increasing frequency, and if at the
critic's desk the scales are tilted against music, in the
ear of the public the balance goes all the other way.
Every great concert is a challenge. Six times a week
there pour out of the Queen's Hall, all through the
summer season, a thousand persons who, in different
degree according to their different capacities, have
experienced a spiritual rapture. When, we must ask,
in the world's history has a vision of life, splendid,
ample, and sublime, like that which Beethoven's Fifth
Symphony unrolls, been a familiar popular possession,
unless it be with the Greeks at Athens when their
great plays were performed? The *Messiah* itself,
though not an artistic unity, though marred by long
tracts of decorative trimming and conventional parade,
has shown serenity and majesty to thousands where
Milton speaks to tens. Bach's great Mass will soon
be a national institution. Its central choruses, culminating in the Sanctus, are religion incarnate ; all
the power and all the associations of words pale into
insignificance before these torrents of reviving sound.
By the test of emotional transfiguration, the power
of art to seize, lift, and transform us, the Mass in
B minor must be pronounced unapproachable, supreme.

This supremacy is only not recognized at present because recognition is verbal, because the enjoyment of music, though commoner in fact than the enjoyment of poetry, can still be regarded as a peculiarity among us, requiring a ' gift ', and because, the development of one gift being apt to be accompanied by the neglect of others, musicians are too often dumb or absent-minded witnesses who allow the verdict to go against them by default. Yet that very tendency which the musician shows—to concentrate on music—is but another evidence of the peculiar magic of the art. What are we to think, then? As music widens its sway, is our whole people to be bewitched by it? Such a consummation (despite the efforts of the British Music Society) does not appear to be immediately likely, but is it to be wished? More seriously, what part can music be expected to play in our developing culture, and how are we to relate it, how should we hope to see it related, to our poetry, that abiding glory of our race? The need for a comparative criticism is only the greater because the claims of our poetry are so strong. But it is of importance to the future of poetry, as of music also, if both are to have the influence and the appreciation proper to them, that neither should be exalted at the other's expense, and in particular that neither should be praised for qualities in which the other easily surpasses it. It would be futile for a young man's mentor, who should wish to dissuade him from indulgence in the pleasures of love, to argue that intenser gratifications of the senses were to be found elsewhere : he would have to say that other gratifications were more interesting and more diversified. Music is to poetry as pleasure to life. Let us not therefore insist excessively upon the delights of poetry, since these are subtle and diffused ; let us dilate rather upon its emancipations, its illuminating power.

If a soberer attitude is required of the criticism of
poetry, how shall we describe what is required of
criticism in music, and how can we hope to modify
an activity which as yet hardly exists?   In its active
and immediate imaginative appeal music grips us
as words are powerless to do.   When a bird utters
its alarm cry, every creature within earshot cowers,
and it is characteristic of all expression to which
emotion gives form that its effect is as sure as an echo.
But the bird only announces that there is cause for
fear, it does not explain what cause ; and the intensely
vivid language of music has a similar limitation, for
the acute and fluctuating emotions which it evokes
are objectless.   Because they are so, we are easily
reduced to the belief that music has no meaning
beyond itself, and that, having called upon us to love
or fear or exult, it has done so for no reason other than
that of the pleasure of an emotional indulgence.
Indeed, there can be no doubt that the effect of music
commonly goes no farther : we yield contentedly to
the stream of pleasure, and mistake the enjoyment
of being borne along by it for the end and the
justification of the art.

We do not accept such an account of it when it
is accompanied by words.   The effect of Brahms's
music, for example, in the opening of the sixth chorus
of his Requiem is to lift us from the realm of allusion,
in which the words alone would leave us, and to
impress us with a convincing sense of realities.   'Here
have we no continuing city, howbeit we seek one to
come ' ; 'we shall not all sleep when He cometh,
but we shall all be changed' : the words, though
winged by poetry, appeal still to our reflection ; to hear
their music with them is to set out on the pilgrimage,
to enter the world as it will be when the mysterious
change has come about.   What, then, would the effect
of the same music be without the accompaniment of

any words ? Its solemnity and tranquillity in strangeness would remain to suggest that its concern was with the ultimate destiny of the soul : and yet, if we heard it at a time when lighter associations were engaging us, and particularly if it were rendered without reference to its larger implications, we could apply it without offence to many a Lilliputian transformation scene. It is because it is set to poetry that its associations are fixed and its emotional bearing relieved of mere intensity and brought to a decisive focus.

Where, then, are the events and objects to which we can attach, in reality, emotions equivalent to those which music arouses in us? We cannot listen long to modern works without being aware how much the more sophisticated composers of the day are haunted by this question ; and it is here surely that the true function of musical criticism is to be found—we mean, in the relating of musical experience to the general experience of life, even to the extent of explaining composers to themselves, by bringing their work before the bar of an enlightened common sense. For the composer, in his abnormal responsiveness and exuberance, is apt both to see more than exists and to say more than he intends ; he attaches to the circumstances of his experience or the creatures of his imagination feelings which transcend alike these creatures and these circumstances. He better than any one knows that music means something, though he may be the last to be able to say what it means. What, after all, is the impulse to write to a programme but the attempt to capture and to cage this elusive meaning, to secure the aid of words and yet to escape the encumbrance of a chorus? And what is the main rock of offence in all descriptive writing, if not its extravagance : that the means so hugely and preposterously overshadow the end? As soon as it ceases to be humorous, as soon as ever it pretends to engross the hearer in those mounting tides of suggestion which flow unsolicited out of the deep ocean of sound, descriptive music has overreached itself : its puny figures, caught on the open sands, are swiftly and pitilessly enveloped and submerged, to disappear from our sight with futile and fantastic gestures.

A true and vital school of musical criticism implies, of course, a public capable of appreciating the issues to be judged, and it is too often supposed that these issues belong to the technique of the art. But technical issues, though particularly afflicting, have no more importance in music than elsewhere ; in a humane appreciation of poetry scansion goes by the board, and so with music do modes and keys and modulations. They are for the workshop. If the music critic talks of sharps and flats, it is not because he has anything of importance to say about them, but because he has nothing of importance to say about anything else. The basis of the critical understanding of music must be, as with that of poetry, an understanding of the human soul ; and since poetry is man's chief externalization of what he is, the criticism of music and poetry must, in fact, always go hand in hand.

How, then, are we to define the relations of music and poetry as the critic or the critical public might best envisage them? It would seem that the mind of man is of a nature to assimilate itself to the universe ; we belong to the world ; the whole is mirrored in us. Therefore, when we bend our thought on a limited object, we concentrate faculties which are naturally endowed with infinite correspondences ; and the response we make to any circumstance of our life is only just, so far as we retain with the feeling of the part the feeling of the whole. Poetry and music alike take cognizance of the interplay in all emotion of part and whole—the subject on one side, with its universal responsiveness, on the other the object, the partial and particular occasion; but their methods are complementary. Poetry works from without inwards; it presents to us as in a glass such objects as in real life might have moved us; it takes life and imprints it upon the soul. Music works from within outwards; its patterns, instead of being imprinted in the listening soul, are drawn up out of it into a relief. We feel and we do not know what we feel, since what we feel is what we are. Our anchor line is cut, and we are adrift upon a tide of universal experience in which the quality of all that we have known is resumed and of all that we are capable of knowing anticipated. The musician takes our whole experience, actual and potential, as the ground of his appeal. In the freedom of his disembodied world he creates types and analogies of emotion which intensify our perceptive power, affecting us more intimately, leading us to a surer self-knowledge, than any experience limited to an event. Only let him remember that the price of the intensification is the detachment. So long as he is content to express a spiritual development, he may wander from his theme, he cannot exaggerate its significance; for it is a theme in which all significances are included.

Is music then to remain for us a mere reminiscence and foretaste of the undefinable? It must do so, but for the fact that, in addition to music, supplementing its impressions and solidifying them for us, we have poetry. We have been searching for an ideal school of musical criticism; we have been wondering what the effect is finally to be of that dazzling apparition, the modern orchestra. The truer our understanding of poetry, the more readily will both these disquietudes be stilled. Poetry has been called a criticism of life; in another sense, more incidentally but not less truly, it may be called a criticism of music. If it be true, on the one hand, that the raptures to which poetry summons us music makes real, it is not less true, on the other, that our enjoyment of them is fruitless while it is left, as music would leave it, unexplained, inexplicable. For the explanation it is to poetry that we must turn ; and when all is said, the best ground for a belief in the future of English music lies in the greatness of English poetry. In that poetry the common experience of our race has been renewed and irradiated. Our poets have built up for us an ideal world after the pattern of the world in which we live ; we have learned from them to transfer our feelings from the one to the other, to assimilate our vision to theirs, applying their ideal to our real and rising so above the limitations of our short-sightedness. The more human consciousness unfolds and its different activities take stock one of another, the more it will be found that, for the sustainment of music at its cloudless height and in all the purity of its removal, there is needed the interpenetrating power of poetry. Poetry and music, for ever irreconcilable, are for ever inseparable too. Seeing them together, we must acknowledge that the meaning of a poem and of a composition have never coincided, never can coincide. Seeing them apart, we must yet recognize that all that music means is all that poetry has said and is to say.

May 1923.

IV

AN ARISTOCRACY OF SERVICE

FEW episodes in literature are more moving than Prince Myshkin's harangue in the Epanchins' drawing-room at the soirée when his betrothal with Aglaia is announced. The Prince, having inherited a large fortune, has been subjected to a long siege by a band of Nihilists who believe him to be as simple as he is rich. He has emerged from the ordeal harassed and torn. Simple indeed he is, being called the Idiot even by his creator, but his simplicity is of that penetrating kind which defeats conspiracy through childlike trust. The violence of the revolutionaries is powerless before his sympathy and patience. He has revealed them to themselves as so many ailing children, and they have become his devoted, remorseful friends. But he himself, though he forgives all and smiles upon the culprits, has not what a contemporary writer calls the technique of forgiveness. It is a joy to him to forgive, but to obtain that joy he has to pass through crises of moral anguish, a kind of vicarious acceptance of the guilt he pardons. And so, though he has a genius for happiness, he is in constant torture, and this torture is a mystery and perplexity to him. 'I know that talking is of little value,' he says, after four pages of talk, to a genial and corpulent member of the higher bureaucracy, while Aglaia and the Epanchins wonder why the earth does not open and swallow them all,

and that the best preaching is example—indeed, I have begun already. But tell me, is it really possible for a man to be unhappy in this world ? You know, I do not understand how any one can walk past a tree and not be happy to see it ; speak to a man, and not be happy to love him. Oh ! unluckily,

G

I do not know how to express myself, but at every step, see, how many lovely things there are which impose their charm even on the most distracted man ! Look at a child, look at the dawn, look at the growing grass, look into the eyes which look at you and love you.

Bruised by the wrongs of men, the Prince has been suffering still acuter torment from a burden of tragic love ; and this very evening, when the Epanchins are receiving him into their family and the world seems ready to smile, he has been reminded anew of his ineffectiveness and shamed before his beloved Aglaia by a careless and fateful gesture. Carried away by his subject—and had she not implored him to forbear sermonizing that one evening at least ?—he had over-turned and broken a great Chinese vase, one of the treasures of the family ; and it seemed to him that his life and all it stood for lay with it in shattered fragments on the floor. In his simplicity of heart he expects these men and women of the *grand monde* to treat him with the scornful reprobation he feels himself to have deserved. But no ! all about him the guests, who had seemed a little stiff while he was lecturing them, are now beaming, and he feels in the air as it were an infection of the warmth and charity which are the breath of his life. It was a mistake, then, to suppose that these people were the enemies of progress, that the sources of the spiritual life were dry in them, that they were ' walking phantoms, exquisite exteriors covering rottenness and lies '. He had misunderstood the Nihilists : their violence was only a perversion of their passion for justice, and if they believed in destruction, it was because belief of some kind was necessary to them, and that the true objects of belief had been removed from their sight. And now, how clearly he saw it, he had misunderstood the ruling classes too. In them, too, was the same fund of human goodness ; they, too, were men who knew how to

understand and how to forgive. He had only to speak
to them and explain the country's need. They had
yet in their hands means to avert the coming disaster.
It surely could not be that holy Russia herself would
one day totter and fall as the vase had fallen. The
barriers were down now; he was at one with his
hearers; his moment had come.

And so there falls from his lips a searching revelation
of social truth. They too, he tells them, with their
frivolities and vanities, are like the rest of mankind;
and for them too, as for the rest, their very faults will
be of service once they are recognized, for they will
become a ground of reconciliation. Yes, it is really
better to be ridiculous sometimes, because mutual
forgiveness becomes easier.

It is impossible to understand everything at once, we do not
reach perfection at the first stroke. To attain to it, it is first
necessary to fail of understanding many things. For if we
understand too fast, we do not understand completely. Yes,
it is to you I say this, to you already so rich in understanding—
and in misunderstanding, too. At present I have no fear for
you. For you know how to forget, you know how to pardon
those who have offended you, no less than those who have been
guilty of no wrong; this last is the most difficult forgiveness.
To pardon those who have given us no offence, that is to say,
to pardon them their innocence and the injustice of our griev-
ances against them. That is what I look for from our nobility,
and it is in the interest of our common safety that I speak.
Why disappear and make way for others, when by becoming
leaders of progress, we can remain leaders of society? Let us
march in the van, and men will follow us. Let us become the
servants of mankind to be its chiefs.

These words are not without their relevance to our
situation in England at the present time; and that
is why we quote them at this season of the New Year
when custom bids us take stock of the past and the
future and strengthen our hearts by conscious resolution. Prince Myshkin's counsel to the Russians was
given half a century ago; it was not heard; and the

great vase, a civilization's treasure, has fallen in irretrievable ruin. There is no immediate parallel between the Russian situation and our own ; and yet we all are conscious that a certain heritage of beauty, and of how much more than beauty, is in danger everywhere. Russia has been the scene of a terrific explosion. The fabric of her Government had become identified with an attempt to suppress certain spiritual forces, which were at work among the people like a fermenting leaven ; a moment came when the pressure from within was greater than the strength of the containing metal, and the whole was blown into the air. England has nothing similar to show. Nevertheless, we recognize that forces similar to those which have brought disaster to Russia are present in the midst of us, and indeed that a certain transformation of life and particularly of the order of life of men in their communities, which has descended upon Russia in a whirlwind, is due to occur in every country of the West. That change can perhaps best be expressed in brief by the suggestion, or shall we say by the admission, that, as the French Revolution marked the disappearance from society of the conception of a divinely ordained *noblesse,* so the Russian Revolution marks the disappearance of the less clearly definable prerogative of the middle class. Who would deny that property, if it has not been fully deified, has at least had its halo among us ? Well, the angels are long gone out of the picture, and the saints must now go too. From to-day forward we are all to be plain men together. Here and everywhere we are witnessing the advent to power of the masses of the people.

The first Revolution in France was followed, as we know, by a number of others ; and the political temper of the French people has never completely thrown off the Revolutionary virus ; French government is still unstable. But the ideas which produced revolution in France were derived from England, and here they brought no upheaval; a way was found to express them in an orderly development. Thus, to her enormous advantage, England retained her nobility, while France lost hers; and by general admission the land of liberty is the land where liberty and nobility remain reconciled and united, not that in which they have been divorced. To say that the ideas of the Russian revolutionaries are, in their turn, derived from England would be absurd; yet in a secondary and deeper sense it would be true. England and her Empire provide the world with so conspicuous an example of free institutions that, wherever peoples rise, let them take their motto where they will, the incentive comes from us, for it is we who have held out before them the irresistible magnet of spiritual freedom. Of course the attempt to organize a nation without that element of ballast which a propertied class provides is even more fantastic than to refuse recognition to the law of heredity. Russia is making the attempt; and though she cannot for long continue to kill by torture every citizen convicted of a balance at the bank, it may yet well be that a hundred years hence the average Russian will still maintain that property disqualifies its possessor for participation in public life and relegates him as a back number, just as the average Frenchman of to-day still excepts the human family from the laws of breeding. The peculiar menace of the present time is that the ideas invoked by revolutionaries are so patently absurd and yet are proving so immensely potent. This means, again, that the crisis is one in which our country is peculiarly called on to lead the world. For it is not in our nature to be attracted by ideas in their bare intellectual form, even when the ideas are good ones; and there is no reason to fear, therefore, that we shall be seduced by bad ideas. Our genius is for action, for the concrete truth. And as we avoided revolution when France succumbed, and to this day retain the idea and fact of a hereditary nobility as a vital principle of our national life, so now, when destructive analysis is attacking a much deeper social principle, who can doubt that it is for us again to find a practical rejoinder, to demonstrate the falsity of the new as of the old abstractions by *living otherwise*, and in the meantime to incorporate into our lives the new forces which are arising in the world and the new truths they bring?

New forces and new truths have indeed to be reckoned with, but will these after all prove compatible with what the human race commands already of truth and force? We cannot assume it, and obviously the element of force is much more conspicuous than the element of truth in the new movements that are confronting us. It is for this reason that the word ' revolution ' is on all our tongues. Human civilization in its successive stages might be likened to a house of cards. The first storey is easily built, or at any rate easily rebuilt when the lesson of building it has once been learned. Then the second storey, if the first has been securely laid, often stands well. But the higher the castle goes, the more perilous is its condition, while yet the impulse to add to it grows more and more imperious. Happy children, innocent of the least notion of equilibrium, hurry forward with beautiful contributions all their own, or take cards from the bottom to add them at the top ; and soon nothing remains but a formless heap upon the floor. In our own case, whether we will or no, the time has come for the addition of a new storey to the pile. Not only so ; the stern laws of this human architecture decree that we must lift the whole work and place it upon new foundations : the addition is not to be from above, but from below.

Yet what is wrong, a reader may ask, and why should there be change or subversion? Has not the much-vaunted democracy finally arrived, and is it not firmly established among us? Who can desire to see a change, when what we have is what the mass of the people themselves have declared they want? Are there not now wider facilities for education, a higher level of comfort, and even a more general diffusion of human kindliness, than have ever existed in the world before? How can we, then, work otherwise than as we are working now; what have we to do but to perfect what is already so admirable? The point of view is not unnatural, but it is not true English, because it does not square with the facts. The fact of the moment is the immense pressure from beneath; and the cause of that pressure, we very well know, is the gathering reaction of human wills against material hindrances, against a confinement which either is or seems arbitrary and unjust. And indeed, though our people govern, they do not yet know that they govern, or what government implies. They vote, but their vote is not fully effective. Power is in their hands, but they do not understand or feel the use of it; as yet they have not even learned its limitations. Their lives are still ordered by what remains of an earlier régime. Our magistrates are Tory, our county councils Tory, our district and parish councils, except in so far as they are Tory, nugatory. The ill-housed miners, burning with their wrongs, had in their hands the machinery for redressing them, but its wheels were clogged. The whole instrument is a survival, and it survives because it has been and in many respects still is so serviceable. But a growing cleavage divides it from the corporate life of which it professes to be a function. Order is benevolently dictated to the people from above. They remain strangers to the processes by which they are ruled. And thus, though all that the people could ask has been given to them, a real danger faces us, in that the forms have been given without the spirit. We have still to apply, we have still, it may be, to discover, the spirit that is appropriate to these new forms.

We are at a crisis of history, and all our strength, all our devotion, are required of us. Democracy has indeed arrived ; that is the whole gist of the matter. The time for talking about it, for believing in it or disbelieving in it, has gone by. It is as useless to cry out against democracy as to cry out against electricity or steam or the laws of dynamics. Perhaps we should be happier if we were Greeks of the Homeric age or mediaeval artists or craftsmen. The very thought is idle. Knowledge has advanced, and we must carry its burden. We must find the happiness appropriate to the conditions of our time. The mind that dreams to-day of paternal government, or any kind of irresponsible direction from on high, stands to the true issue in politics where followers of Ruskin used to stand in the struggle against machinery. Democracy is here, with all its hopes and perils, and only one kind of political thought is now pertinent—the thought which is addressed to solving the tremendous problems it involves. It is a little as if we had been given wings and the internal combustion engine and told to fly. Only we might have declined the venture in that case, and in this we cannot. The risks are terrible and they are inevitable. Once printing was invented, the day was due to come when every man alike would claim the privileges and responsibilities of manhood, of which citizenship is the chief. And now we have to organize a community through which the consciousness of citizenship may pulse without a check, every member of which may feel he has some point of living contact with the powers that move and guide the whole.

We spoke of a cleavage in our political organization between the spirit and the forms. There is a con-

spicuous sign of it ; it is the advent of a Labour
Party. Nothing surely can be more obvious than that
in a country where democracy was in effective operation
no Labour Party could arise. For political aims will
never be served by division into non-political factions.
If then such a division has occurred among us, we are
forced to recognize in that event the workings of
a kind of Nemesis. Had not our rulers neglected in
earlier days interests which a more enlightened
patriotism would have striven to promote, it would
have been impossible for the working classes to band
themselves together now and to take that very neglect
for their foundation. Here then, it would seem, we
have a suggestion for the first step towards readjust-
ment ; and it involves at once what Prince Myshkin
calls the most difficult forgiveness. It is a misfortune
politically that there should be a Labour Party,
because the cohesion of such a party rests upon no
principle. What we desire in those whom we elect
to govern us is not that they shall be members of one
or of another class, but that they shall be men with
whose ideas we sympathize and whose character we
believe to have been formed by training and experience
to meet the responsibilities of high position. We
recognize, too, that all education has a hereditary
element—that a fully educated man is, with rare
exceptions, the product of at least three generations.
The work of government being of that most complex
kind which demands of a man that he shall not only
be educated, but unconscious of his education—a
further refinement—, it can never be possible to
recruit large numbers of such men from among the
manual workers of the country. We are therefore
grieved with the Labour Party for existing, and more
and more grieved as we follow the more and more
striking development of its successes ; for all our
admiration for many of its leaders cannot blind us to

the fact that such men are and always must be exceptional. Yet our grievance is unjust, and so far as there is a grievance anywhere, it lies against the other elements of the country—those which, in their handling of the political weights, have excluded the workers from consideration and furnished them with a negative principle for cohesion where no positive principle could have been found ; and our first task is to recognize the innocence of Labour and the injustice of our griefs against it.

The next point, surely, to be recognized is that, having accepted the democratic principle for our country, having but lately accorded the whole of the machinery required for its realization, we have cleared the ground for a swift walk-over by those very forces which we are yet disposed to regard as revolutionary. Our political apparatus, as it stands, is formed to make the voice of the masses effective and dominant ; yet the surprise, verging sometimes upon consternation, with which the growth of a people's party is regarded would suggest that power was accorded nominally, as if in the hope or dream that nominal power would suffice and that the holders would never come forward to exchange the name for the reality. That change is now rapidly taking place ; and though it is in one sense, if only because of its rapidity, a revolutionary change, it will never with us proceed by revolutionary methods, unless, persisting in old errors, we attempt to twist against the people's will the machinery we have devised for its expression. Sooner or later, we may be assured, forces resembling those we now call Labour will overflow the House of Commons and possess themselves of both sides of it. To struggle as against an impending menace, to play for time by tricks and sops and subterfuges, in the hope of strengthening the outworks and turning or weathering the tornado when it comes, is futile policy. Perhaps for the near future our choice lies between two alternatives : a Parliament in which the popular forces are opposed to the rest of the community, with an ever-increasing preponderance of weight on their side ; or one in which the true representation of the masses is accepted as a primary function of both parties, to such a degree that all further distinction of Labour from the rest of the community becomes impossible. However we approach it, and whether the way be rough or smooth, our task is the reintegration of our whole national organism. For the weightiest and most potent of its elements is at present the least operative. And we shall know when we have won through. It will be when the old and true distinctions have re-established themselves, when the time-honoured opposition of Conservative and Progressive rules once more.

Such is our present situation, and it imposes on us as difficult a duty as that to which Prince Myshkin summoned his friends the Russian bureaucrats as they sat smiling over the spilt fragments of the broken vase. The high idealism of his words befits the season. No one has yet imagined a mission campaign to save the souls of politicians, and yet what is most necessary in politics is a change of heart, and we are beginning to preach it. And if we say politicians, we do not mean alone or principally those to whom the label is attached. We must all be politicians if our country is to survive, and what is more, we must be democrats ; above all—and here is the first sign of conversion !—nowhere tolerating charity as a substitute for justice and independence. Complete personal independence for every Englishman, with economic independence, of course, for its foundation-stone—that must be our constant aim ; and then, that this independence everywhere learn its political rights and responsibilities, beginning where they work most modestly, near home. We have all seen the great well at Carisbrooke Castle : there is an image of democracy in the court-yard. To get water, you do not press a button; you harness the donkey; and he, fumbling and stumbling, turns the enormous wheel and brings up a meagre pailful. The democratic wheel is just as cumbrous, and it has to be turned. So it is a case of harness for every one : we must champ the bit of the parish council, or even of the women's institute.

The special need of the day is still the need which Myshkin proclaimed : leaders for the people, leaders who will understand that acceptable leadership implies, and now more than ever implies, willingness to serve. Much has already been asked of the English upper classes, and in no country of the world is the sense of duty and responsibility attaching to leadership so high. We know the saying ' To him that hath shall be given ' ; it has a corollary, ' He that hath given much shall give more ', and the last gift required of our leaders is a kind of self-effacement. There never was a time when leadership was needed more, and one reason why we so greatly feel the need is that few understand the terms on which alone it can be effectively given. If in the future we are to be led aright, we must be led by those very elements, if not by those very classes, which lead us now. We must have men of rank, men of culture, men of the world to captain us. But while the men must be the same, their leadership must be different, it must be differently conceived and applied. He alone can lead to-day who will stoop to be chosen for a leader ; who will take the pains to make his leadership desired. He must recognize that prescriptive rights of property, position, education, though in one sense they qualify him, in another disqualify him for his task. They separate him from the people, they surround him with an atmosphere of mystery, they are obstacles to be surmounted. And there is only one power that can surmount these obstacles—human sympathy, the sense of comradeship, love. For our country's sake the privileged must put their privileges aside, the wealthy must become poor in spirit, and, that they may still lead the people, must become as brothers among them.

At any other time than this such a demand would be fantastic, for the leopard does not change his spots. Yet there are signs to-day 'that he is changing them. We did not need the war to teach us that Englishmen love their country better than their lives. The same great love continues working now under conditions more calculated to obscure it. The spirit of generosity and sacrifice still lives, and it is plain to-day that many love their country better than their possessions. High spiritual qualities disclose themselves even among the aridities and calculations of parliamentary debate, and men take courage at their apparition, as if they should have seen the city pavement put forth flowers. There is a conscious deepening of the national life, and it would seem as if, in this fateful hour, our people were already possessed of the knowledge that can save them. Though property is everywhere under attack, it is not with us the principle that is in question. Every Englishman knows that private possessions, and even privileges of a kind, are essential elements in the national life. Indeed, this is so fully recognized, so strong is the fundamental sanity of our people, that property has no need to be nursed and protected artificially, as it too often has been in the past ; it can be trusted to take care of itself. Let us resolve therefore to clear ourselves of any suspicion of the reproach that we care less for the souls of men than for their appanages. Our social order is safe just in so far as we can translate its values into terms of human life. The ultimate values are human values always ; the sanctions of property itself are secondary ; our last claim to our possessions is that we hold them for the common good.

1 *January* 1920.

V

'RECONSTRUCTION'

IT was a turning-point in human history when the first tool was invented; the condition of mind to which the thought of sharpening a stone revealed itself is irrecoverable now. Yet similar revelations are dawning upon one or other of us daily; for we live in an age of invention. The human organism is continually taking to itself new limbs; we have. come to perceive that the whole world is man's tool-box and that one of the aims of his life here is to learn its uses.

In spite of the mind's natural haughtiness and the spirit's distaste, there is no avoiding the conclusion that a progressing material organization is essential to spiritual advance. Our ears are deafened with the whirr of turning wheels, but out of the hubbub itself there arises a summons, telling us of a good to be attained, a vision which we must reach after. In other ages, and elsewhere even in this age, generations pass, the old tools serve, and life runs in a placid, even circle. Contentment becomes a convention, limitations clothe themselves in beauty, and the wheel is a symbol of infinity in equipoise, so that prayer itself turns on a wheel. For us the wheel still symbolizes infinity; but it also, it mainly, symbolizes progress.

Yet it would be fatal if we were to forget that rapid material developments jeopardize our civilization, that an epoch like the present contains germs of evil capable of overthrowing the whole fabric that humanity has so laboriously built up. The material instrument is impersonal, as likely in itself to destroy life as to promote it; it has no inherent value save that of stimulating the intelligence which it is to serve. It imposes a problem which we must solve or perish. The more tools we employ the more complex our world becomes, and the more agile must be the mind that is to make such a world its home : the more agile and the more stable too. It seems at times that our task of keeping up with our discoveries has reduced us already to an all but desperate plight ; we might compare contemporary humanity to a conjurer with all his balls in the air, while a malicious Pierrot beside him keeps tossing up fresh ones. We only profit by all this excitement in so far as we succeed in applying it constructively. New conditions of life are born of it and a new burden of responsibility. The question is whether the conscience of the race, its taste, its judgement, and its wisdom are keeping pace with its intelligence.

Never was the issue more momentous than it is to-day, when, the war being over, the nations of the world are setting forth to lay the foundations of an epoch. The crisis involved a concentration of the whole of our spiritual activities on the attainment of one object. We emerge from the war, therefore, more familiar than ever with the material possibilities at our command, and also with a certain intensification of pre-existing habit and routine in our attitude to them. There is more than common danger that we may be caught up in our own machinery, because the significance of life has been for so long compressed into the terms of a material issue. What, after all, is to be the outcome of the enormous material expansion which we are witnessing in our western civilization ? Whither are we tending ?

The question has been acutely before us as we read and pondered over M. Édouard Herriot's *Créer*.[1]

---

[1] *Créer*. Par Édouard Herriot. Two volumes. (Paris : Payot. 11 f.)

M. Herriot, the popular Mayor of Lyons, is less a
writer than a man of action, or, rather, he is one
of those many-sided natures for whom literature is
a way of entry into the wider life of affairs. His
style has in consequence a quality of fibrous tensity
and perhaps also a certain terseness or impatience, as
though it was an indignity for a man to scratch with
a pen when he might be moulding and hammering
and shaping forth his thought in the living material.
It was characteristic of M. Herriot to have conceived
and accomplished *en pleine guerre* (it is one of his
favourite locutions) the organization at Lyons of a
great industrial and commercial fair. He recognized
that the blockade gave French enterprise a unique
opportunity ; he had at once the strength and the
faith to seize the favourable moment, and the first
Foire des Échantillons opened under his presidency at
the time of the most agonizing uncertainties of the
battle of Verdun. But M. Herriot's distinction does
not rest only on his boldness of initiative and his
driving power as a constructive administrator. He
unites with these a remarkable suavity, and his dealings
with men are illumined not only by a wide and generous
benevolence but also by gifts of intuition which his
training in literature has at once fortified and refined.
No Englishman present at the celebration of Empire
Day in Lyons in 1918, no Oxford man who then heard
M. Maurice Barrès explain, with frequent quotation
from Mr. H. G. Wells, what England, and in particular
what Oxford, was, will forget the emotion of solace he
experienced when M. Herriot rose ; he had only to
propose the dispatch of a congratulatory telegram to
the Prime Minister, but his choice of words had
a restoring virtue which disposed of a thousand
unfortunate impressions.

   It is natural that such a man should wish to do
for his whole country in time of peace what he has

already done for his city in time of war. Such, in a sentence, is the gist of *Créer*. The Lyons Fair was a challenge to Leipzig. In *Créer* M. Herriot sounds a rallying cry to the whole French people. He demands immediate steps in every department of the national life towards the reorganization and re-establishment of French power and prosperity, and, above all, towards the provision of the necessary material foundations. We shall not be so injudicious as to criticize the details of the exhaustive programme he sketches out, but shall content ourselves with saying that the eminence of France, which is his care, is the care of the whole civilized world, and that, according to our conception, it was a primary object of the war to assure it.

But what is the main road to national eminence at the present time ? M. Herriot has no hesitation whatever in pronouncing. It is industrial organization and efficiency, a unified and scientific direction of the nation's energy towards material production ; he would have France one vast factory. He indicates a number of means for the attainment of this ideal—development of harbours and marine, organization of canals and riverways, agricultural reform, colonial expansion, a new credit system, and so forth—but his emphasis falls on the necessity of universal technical education, of higher and higher practical specialization for the masses, and not for the masses only ; for even the *élite*, who reach a university, are to be trained primarily for research. *Comprendre et créer*. Knowledge, says M. Herriot, must everywhere displace routine, and men's practice must be directed, not by the accidents of their experience (*l'empirisme*), but by scientific theory based on exhaustive prevision of the entire range of relevant fact. There are to be training schools for everybody ; there are to be training schools even for waiters in hotels.

For *le tourisme* is not only *un sport*, it is a factor also of ever-increasing commercial value. France, indeed, possesses already a waiters' training school, with an ' education ' comprising nine sections, of which M. Herriot gives us the list : (1) stenography and typewriting ; (2) foreign languages and customs ; (3) geography from a traveller's point of view ; and so on. Those who wish to visit France must be quick about it or these waiters will have matriculated. They have no terrors for M. Herriot. He even foresees a time when the Loire will compete with the Rhine in its organization of hotels and steamboats, and become a correctly exploited pleasure highway. He will be content so long as all the waiters are French and all the gains go into French pockets. The law of modern industry, says M. Herriot, is concentration or national unification of programme, with science directing equally the conception and the execution of the work to be done. He sees all modern nations evolving towards an industrial type, and is confident that the philosophy of industrialism, however it may work out in its details, will be found ultimately to repose on this foundation. And the motive power of the whole movement is always national greatness. We are to be progressively ' taylorized ' in order, if we are French, that we may produce more than the Germans ; or, if we are English, that we may produce more than the French. For, obviously, to be great a nation must be a power in the world, and power depends on production.

Up to a certain point it is all obvious and irrefutable. But we soon reach this point ; and is it not when we have passed beyond it that the questions arise which are most worth answering and which at this particular crisis of human history demand an answer ? What, we cannot but ask ourselves, was the significance of the war, what is the significance of our victory, if we can so soon forget that great protest which came from the very heart of humanity against a threatened subjugation of the mind? Whether you beat your neighbour by militarism or buy him by industrialism, the action is the same and the effect is the same, if once you have accepted slavery as a means to it. And slavery begins wherever the spontaneous action of the developing mind comes to an end. The peril of industrialism is simply that it deadens the mind; and like militarism, it works its deadly effect in two ways. There is a kind of hypnotic influence exercised by the whole great mechanism, and in the thought of the power it represents, so that men are imperceptibly led on to use it for the sake of using it, and for the sake of the pleasure they have in feeling a huge force in motion under their hands. This is the peril for the few; while, for the many, there is the dulling influence of monotonous lives, the mind being attacked not directly, as in the old military drill, but indirectly by the absence of any occasion for its exercise. It is perhaps because M. Herriot has succumbed more than he is aware to the first influence that he seems to appreciate so little the dangers which are involved in the second. In England, once called the garden of the world, though we are far indeed from any grip of the problem, we yet are bitterly aware, if only through the conspicuous and advancing defacement of our sweet countryside, that the problem exists, and that we must one day face it. Our factory system began so early that the need for control of industrial conditions which we now feel so intensely was necessarily perceived too late. Meantime not the face of our country alone, but the physique of our people has suffered terribly, and with their physique their intellectual and moral fibre. It is true that our vast commercial expansion has served to make our name great in the world; but from day to day it becomes more evident to us that this greatness, so far as it rests on industrialism, rests insecurely. For industrialism, as we have so far developed it, involves a vast population of over-specialized, strained, discontented machine-men; and upon human material of this kind, we know very well, a great empire cannot be maintained.

The question, then, as we apprehend it, is not whether or to what extent you shall industrialize, but *how*; and, since competition between nations is destined for many generations to be the spur to effort, the great prize will fall surely to that nation which first organizes what we might call the practical reconciliation of industrialism with enlightenment and with humanity. The makeshift growths we see around us carry the seed of dissolution. Industrialism is a function of society; but in its present forms it produces men who do not understand the primary laws of social life, and these very men are coming forward in their millions to assume the direction of affairs. It is clear that the pressing practical need is not to be the quickest, but to be the surest. The organization of a super-scientific trade is of secondary moment; what is of the first moment is the diffusion of humane enjoyments.

France is much more favourably situated than we are for the solution of the problem in its most serious aspects. A far larger proportion of her people is engaged in agriculture, and so remains in touch with sane and steadying influences, nor has her countryside been sullied by smoke and slime to an appreciable degree. Wherever you go in France you find yourself within walking distance of water that a man can fish in or of trees and grass where he can sit with his family and breathe fresh air. Here is one enormous advantage. We have to remember that a need may not be less imperative because it does not declare itself at stated hours, as do hunger and fatigue. The mind, like the body, has its digestive processes, and even when well nourished will perish of inanition unless certain accompaniments are provided, as poultry do if they are deprived of grit. Commerce with nature and natural beauty is a fundamental need if health is to be maintained through generations; and next in order of urgency comes housing; for if a man is to have the mind of a citizen he must have a citizen's home. Housing has its emotional as well as its utilitarian side. A man requires that his house shall not only be commodious, but that it shall express his nature, that it shall suggest the meaning of his place in the community, in the world. This is true everywhere, but, above all, in towns. The town must atone to its inhabitants for all it robs them of by giving them in exchange clear symbols of the high functions which men unite to pursue. The French town is immeasurably superior to the English in this respect. It will be far easier to introduce sanitation in Lyons than to give nobility to Manchester.

But even where these first two claims are provided for, the industrial worker still remains unbalanced, incomplete, as a result simply of the kind of work he is called upon to do; and the problems inherent in factory life are not touched. This is why education, which has always been a primary need of humanity, is peculiarly and urgently needed now. The occupations of a large number of men are rendering them actively unfit to play their part in the life of the community. The diffusion of ideas gives them at the same time a more and more influential part to play. Disaster awaits the nation that does not find means to complete the manhood of its citizens and to teach them the responsibilities of citizenship. M. Herriot has some charming pages on the subject of education, and we should have liked to quote in full his description of a country schoolhouse where white roses, the variety called Bouquet de Marie, looked in at the window, swaying slowly on their delicate stems, and where the classroom's message, ' Remember ', was echoed by the garden's message, ' Observe '. Yet, perhaps because all institutions are imperfect and because higher education in France, if we are to trust his account of it, is peculiarly so, the futility of the humanities is his main theme and their too common association with classical studies. When, then, shall we all admit that there is one final subject for a true education—human nature itself? If the manner in which the one subject is studied is not abreast of the times, the reason, we should have thought, is that too much of the limited stock of ability available has been diverted to the immediately remunerative fields of applied science. It is M. Herriot's desire that these very fields should be more deeply and more systematically exploited. Surely the cure for our ills lies in the opposite direction. The momentum of things, the blind pull of dead environment, has touched the danger-point, and safety requires us to match one development with another, to redress the balance by becoming intensively and extensively more human. A renaissance of the humanities—that is the great need of the times.

There is a further point. The problems of the spiritual life, the obstacles which the individual soul encounters in its struggle towards perfection, are always of the same kind ; but the problems offered to the mind by the conditions of human life on the earth vary from age to age. Upon the solution we find for them as they successively present themselves depends the clearness with which our common environment is irradiated with spiritual light. Poverty, for example, was in past time a necessary condition for the mass of the people, and with it ignorance. But, scientific invention having now removed this necessity, the persistence of slums, and all they imply, becomes an element of added spiritual darkness. In that respect we have notable arrears to make good. What then is our essentially contemporary problem? Is it not the fact that the machinery we now possess is adequate not only for the diffusion of general well-being but for its establishment on the broadest possible basis, with no frontier but the world's? What has chiefly disappointed us in M. Herriot's book is that he seems, in this respect also, blind to the true signs of the times. To speak quite candidly, the time has come, in his eyes, for France to do, in a French way and with the militarism left out, what Germany was doing before the war. He does not appreciate the dangers besetting his own and every country as the result of the influences we have been describing, and he does not see that the reign of pure nationalism is over. Either the growth of machinery means nothing, or it means the opportunity for an always increasing number of men .to think and feel humanely. Perhaps its most important service is to provide them with better and better facilities for the inter-communication of their thoughts. Viewed thus, our material equipment has indeed an aspect of sublimity. A new period of history is ushered in. The general fellowship of man with man is made possible for the first time. This being so, there can be no stability in the future for any great power rebuilt out of the ruins of the old fabric. The nations can no longer publish Truth and Justice in private editions of their own ; there must be one journal for the world. It is not that thought has changed. The nation will never be less than it is now. The family is not less now, it is more, than in the time when it was the war-unit. Patriotism is as undying as love. Hunger and rivalry remain the motive forces of our material life. Thought has not changed ; but we have new conditions for its fulfilment. That is now possible which was a dream before. Humanity is no longer a merely Utopian word ; it is a realizable idea. We have the means to begin realizing it and, unless we use them, they will turn upon us and destroy us.

July 1919.

VI

AN ASPECT OF THE LEAGUE
OF NATIONS

A FAVOURITE preoccupation among leaders of
practical thought in France during the last century
was that of seeking in the conditions of European
society for foundations on which to build a new
spiritual power—*un nouveau pouvoir spirituel*. With
a sense of tradition not indeed stronger, but very
differently rooted from ours, they recognized instinctively as we do not, as with us only students of history
do, that Europe had fallen away from unity, that she
had been at one time a great family guided by the
Church ; and they saw clearly that there could be
no eventual adjustment of her differences except under
the guidance of some kind of controlling organization
which must, as the Church had done, express primarily
the common strivings of man's nature after an ideal life
and his recognition in the world of presiding Goodness,
and which must, at the same time, become a recognized
part of the temporal order and, in the last resort, wield
a more august and a more effective influence than
temporal governments themselves. M. Émile Faguet,
one of the most eloquent and not one of the least
enlightened exponents of the ever-vital genius of
French criticism, devoted to this theme an admirable
little volume,[1] which might be remembered to-day
if its gifted author had not since its appearance diverted
the attention of his readers with so many other treatises
almost as good. He began with a study of Saint-Simon

[1] *Politiques et Moralistes du XIXᵉ Siècle.* Par Émile Faguet. Deux-
ième Série. (Paris : Société Française d'Imprimerie et de Librairie.
7 f.)

and passed through Lamennais, Quinet, and others to Auguste Comte. Sympathizing deeply with the common purpose of one after another of his protagonists, recognizing that the Catholic Church itself more nearly corresponded still to the object of their enthusiastic dreams than anything they were likely to put up in its place, he showed how in spite of all its crudeness—though perhaps he was not perfectly aware how far that crudeness went—Comte's humanitarianism was the nearest approach an individual had made to a solution of that peculiar *impasse* which is the affliction of our modernity. Comte actually succeeded in founding a religion : in this sense at least, that he attracted an appreciable number of worshippers to a novel shrine. Thousands believed, hundreds believe still, that the age-long rupture between faith and knowledge had been healed, and that man had found a temple to which he could bring his heart and his mind together.

The religion of humanity was a failure ; but there is something to be learned from the degree of relative success which it obtained. Human society has still no greater need than an instrument of universal spiritual guidance, and to us in England who can look upon the prospects and proceedings of the Catholic Church with dispassionate eyes, there seems no likelihood whatever of a new rally around the old creeds. The terrible sufferings and humiliations to which European civilization is committed by the catastrophe of the war will no doubt reveal to multitudes one final source of strength which is independent of material success and failure ; and the desire to believe the Church to be the true depository of life will greatly strengthen. But our English Church itself lags behind in its relation to what we might call the enlightened devotion of the time, and the strength of the Roman Church, if it can be called strength, is to have suspended the thought of spiritual progress altogether. This attitude makes a strong appeal to sophisticated minds ; it avoids disturbance of the unawakened. But the mass of mankind are never to be found in the first of these categories, and they are less and less likely to be found in the second. To simple inquirers the tenets of the Church are lessons in the impossible, and they will assume this character more strikingly as knowledge is more popularized. The result will be an extension of atheistic materialism, already on the Continent far more general, far cruder, and more violent than it is with us.

One great advantage follows from this dethrone- ment of organized religion. Thoughts of a spiritual federation were in the past limited to Europe ; a spiritual power which was not also a Christian power could not then have been conceived ; and there was no appreciable loss in such a limitation at a time when the chief religions had each a world of its own. But now, when all races are in communication and history is one, the case is changed. Indeed, if the truths of Christianity, even in Christian countries, are matters about which men are as much inclined to argue as to agree, their quarrels themselves help them to appreciate the limits of the religious domain and to recognize that differences of religious faith are com- patible with substantial unanimity in regard to the general meaning and purpose of human life. It would seem characteristic of the time, in any case—not- withstanding claims to the possession of ultimate truth which different religious communions advance— to regard the problems of the religious life as pre- dominantly individual and to found the hope of world- wide spiritual co-operation on the desire, now almost universal, to make the world in which we live a better place to live in.

We may go farther and say that a characteristic of the

era is a divorce between the religious and the spiritual. No Church is more liberal than ours ; yet even with us the Church represents on the whole a conventionalized spirituality, while now, as ever, the hallmark of the spiritual is vitality and initiative power The point of radical divergence appears, we think, in relation to what is called the materialism of the age. Our religion, if it accepts science, does not embrace it, and tends to regard the vast fabric of scientific appliances on which our modern life is reared as irrelevant to spiritual development, as at the best a distraction which in its noise and glitter may serve to weary us of vanities. Yet the best effort of the age runs along different, we might even say along more Christian, lines ; for it was of Christ's nature to accept the world. The age is materialistic, and from its materialism we are learning the spiritual value of the material vehicle. One of the chief aims of our devotion is to redeem mankind from the bondage of poverty, and we see that the necessary means to this end is a new material equipment. The more we pursue seemingly material ends, the more we are led to recognize the close interlocking of all the influences to which human life is a response and the interdependence of all human lives on one another. Thus a new route leads us to an old discovery. We become humanitarians once more ; only we see men's brotherhood on its mechanical side and conceive of its realization in terms of coal or oil or electricity. Impelled by a spiritual motive, our action assumes a material bias ; and, conversely, beginning outside the walls of the Church, it leads us to perceive that there is but one Church after all, and that it is the whole human family. Thus there arises, there has arisen, a practical humanitarianism, concentrating its attention on means, methods, machinery, and yet combining with these material preoccupations a growing discernment of the ultimate spiritual issues involved. In fact, a natural co-operation is set up between the two elements necessary to the establishment of a universal spiritual authority.

For, of course, a spiritual power, to be established, must be materialized; the meaning and the purpose have to associate themselves with the mechanism necessary to their fulfilment, with forces of various kinds including those which we politely call sanctions. This comes out very clearly in the thought of the French thinkers to whom we have referred. We see them constantly divided in mind between the love of truth and the desire for its prevalence and establishment, and not so much for its establishment in the minds of men as, so to speak, its establishment over them. They saw the warrings and the fevers to which men are committed when they have only their limited worldly interests to be their guide; and they sought not so much for a means of enlightenment as for a principle of loyalty, which, while it engaged the enlightened, might discipline the rest. The old unity, to which their minds instinctively reverted, was temporal in origin; it was the Roman Empire itself, no less; and later, as the Holy Roman Empire, or the Holy Catholic Church, its pacifying influence, though spiritualized, was temporal still. Here was a vast organization, binding men by palpable links and fetters to a common recognition of Divine truth; and even the most powerful of the earth could not afford to mock the truth at will; for its light was not light only, it was also power. Where, they asked themselves, was such a combination to be looked for in the modern world? How could they effect anew the alliance between power and light?

Their error was in every case the same. The old truths having been dethroned, they wanted to enthrone new ones. They did not see that truth enthrones itself.

If your organization is to be a power, it must be founded not on what men should, but on what they do, believe ; and this granted, the problem of organization which follows will be primarily a mechanical one. For truth cannot be imposed ; even for the most practical purposes its power is its light; and religious truth, as purest light, is least of all imposable. To apply the edicts of God to the coercion of unbelievers would be an impossible anachronism to-day ; it was the monarch of the Philistines who lately became the mouthpiece of Providence. In this respect even men who deny progress must recognize that a sensible advance has been made. The difficulties which spiritual solidarity encounters at the present time do really spring from our finer discrimination of its nature and essence. It was easy enough to organize superstition ; but superstition serves us much less than in the past. The organization of truth is a different thing altogether, since truth cannot be distributed in blocks or swallowed whole. This does not mean that it has become impossible to invoke spiritual laws for the guidance of human affairs, but only that in each department we are confined to the invocation of that part of the law which bears upon it. We conceive of the spirit as an influence bathing the whole world in light and transfusing all things, and our aim is to conduct all our enterprises in that light and to bring each to its characteristic perfection.

The problem of a universal spiritual power presents itself to us therefore in a new aspect. Ceasing to attempt the codification of any body of truth which may one day command the general allegiance of men, leaving the influence of Christ if we are Christians, of Mohammed if we are Mohammedans, of democracy if we are democrats, of Guild Socialism itself if we are Guild Socialists, to grow each by its inherent virtue, we recognize that the first need of the day is collaboration for practical ends, and that the spiritual quality of the collaboration will belong to it, not because it is conducted by prophets, priests, or kings, nor yet because it is associated with any kind of formulated creed, but by virtue simply of the living association of human thought and will it will establish. The time is passing when material forces could be rallied about traditional or revealed ideas ; men think for themselves and will not offer their allegiance and devotion to taught truth. Ideas now reveal themselves in the fabric of our common life. Mere materials even, the dumb, the brutal, convey, if an obvious and primary, yet an intelligible message, so much humbler, and saner, is man now than he used to be. If we lose one conception of the spiritual, a conception our leaders have long accustomed themselves to conjure with, we gain another, and the virtue of this new conception is that its test is action.

The establishment of a controlling spiritual authority in the affairs of the world would seem to turn, therefore, on the question whether we can define a single aim capable of securing the allegiance of men ; or rather not on the question whether we or any one can define such an aim, but on the question whether the course of events and the minds of men have not of themselves defined it. And the question so put answers itself. There hardly exists now in the world a thinking being who is not aware that the forces of destruction at our command are a menace to the growth and development of any consistent meaning in human life. However that meaning may present itself to us, we all agree that it cannot be advanced by the extinction of those in whom it resides. The spiritual, whatever else and more it may be, is first of all simply the living ; and perhaps the whole antagonism of spiritual and material, which in many aspects is so complicated, reduces itself at last practically to this—that the forces

from which our life proceeds can be disposed either
so as to enhance or so as to negate one another. In
proportion as they enhance one another, life becomes
profounder, richer, more intense ; in proportion as
they negate one another, it is reduced to its simplest
elements or disappears. For the time is gone by in
which the struggle for life, meaning by that the struggle
among living things which should live, had spiritual
significance. There is, indeed, a struggle for life still,
and there always must be, but the life for which we
struggle is not mere life any more ; we aim at a
particular kind of life and know that to obtain it and
secure it we must agree together. And the more
meaning life holds, the greater relatively is the menace
of meaningless ·destruction ; while all that is best
worth building, every spiritual achievement that
counts, implies and demands security against the
irruption of blind and alien elements.

Is there not in philosophy a process by which the
things that are are proved inevitable by the pure light
of reason ? We have inscribed the foregoing remarks
to the League of Nations and have aimed at suggesting
that the League has a certain similar inevitability ;
only, our point has been, and it is the strongest aspect
of the case, this inevitability of the League is relative
to the needs and the working influences of the day.
The thought of universal peace is age-old ; schemes
for the establishment of an international tribunal
have been formed again and again ; and the vanity of
the thought of peace, as shown by the failure of all
past efforts to secure it, is one of the commonest
arguments on the lips of opponents of the League—
for in politics there can be no concern except with
what is practicable. We have therefore thought it of
value to point out that mankind was not in the past
ripe for any such organization ; in the first place,
because it demands a mechanical unity, which never

existed before; and, in the second, because it turns upon a conception of the material life as a vehicle of the spiritual which is now for the first time widely prevalent. The Christian religion has, indeed, always idealized peace, but Christians have also proved themselves always the greatest fighters. Even now it is not perhaps entirely an accident that in many countries it is the religious party that is militarist; for it would seem to be one of the dangers of other-worldliness that we relegate the ideal to heaven too easily and are too ready to put up with a compromise in our conduct on this relatively unimportant earth. In the past that has certainly been a difficulty, a difficulty increased, of course, by the palpable impracticability of instituting peace among men.

That impracticability is now disappearing. Indeed, the chief impediment that remains is the survival in men's minds of a sense of impracticability inherited from a different world. What was demonstrably impossible before is demonstrably possible now. In the past men's minds ran ahead of their machinery, it is now the machinery that is running ahead of the minds. They have but to catch up with it, to appreciate the virtue of the instrument which is at their service, and they will find that the way is open at last for the establishment of justice, that there is no reason why the reign of man should not begin.

For obvious reasons we have connected the League of Nations with the humanitarian ideal. But it would be a misfortune if we should forget that to many the word humanitarian has a sickly sound. We have presumed so far that universal brotherhood was admittedly a solid good. The thought of it is also a climax for oratory and its name a password among malcontents and dreamers. We need not do more than refer here to such vacuities, adding, however, this suggestion, that there can be but one end to them; the false and hollow humanitarianism can be superseded only by the sound and true. Curiously enough, some of the most active opponents of the League of Nations are the more ardent Nationalists. They associate the idea of the League not only with the illusions and hypocrisies that prey on minds innocent of the world's affairs, but also with the influences of what is called Internationalism, influences derived from the belief that a man is first Man, after that perhaps a rich man or a poor one, and French or English more or less accidentally and last of all. But, however we approach the League of Nations, whether from the side of methods and organization, or of purpose and significance, we equally see that this particular objection is invalid. It is true that a great many persons, seeing only war and its horrors and connecting them with the rivalry of nations and the intoxications of the national spirit, desire to substitute in men's minds for the sense of loyalty to their nation that of loyalty to their race; but such persons, clearly, have nothing to offer to a League which takes nationality for a starting-point, and they are obviously in error if they suppose that national animosities are the only menace to peace. As for the internationalists of Socialist persuasion, and those who look for a blessing to fall upon the world through the enthronement everywhere of workers representing workers, their contribution is, of course, more negative still. For, in so far as the interests of the workers of different nations are still identical, they are so in view of a common and predominating antagonism, of which accession to power would deprive them; and then there would ensue quarrels more materialistic even than such as the world has seen hitherto, quarrels the destructiveness of which would be intensified by the consternation of inexperience and the pangs of disillusion.

If, then, we connect the League of Nations with

humanitarianism, it is in fullest recognition of the fact that humanitarianism is not only a goal to be attained but also a scourge to be abated, and that in its ignorant and vapid forms it is one of the afflictions of our time. The virtue and working strength of the League, as we conceive it, is that its humanitarianism is constructive and articulate, resting on the perception that we can only become men in the universal sense after due realization of the successive particularities of our manhood. For there is but one enduring principle for the construction of human ties, and it is that which proceeds from within outwards. The wider the circle goes, the more apparent is this truth. We belong to ourselves first, then to our family, then to our city, our county, our country, and finally to the world. And yet, conversely, each time we enlarge the circle we enrich the content of the inner rings. There could be no perfection of individual development until individuals were grouped in common relation to a sovereign society ; and it is the same where nations are concerned. Talk of the sovereignty of national rights is mere obscurantism, bandied about by persons who call themselves realists, and who have in fact never conceived of a nation.as a spiritual entity at all. The first true recognition of national rights, national being, of the very essence and meaning of nationality, can only dawn on the world when nations recognize one another as members of a society whose law they constitute together and bind themselves to obey. There can be no humanity except through nationality ; but our thought of what a nation's life may become is as yet dim because we have never yet perfectly respected it. Nations will begin truly to live when their relative physical strength and stature is of no more importance in the eyes of the world than that of individual men is now.

June 1920.

VII

TOWN HOUSING

In her amusing little book *Latin and Anglo-Saxon* Mrs. Edith Wharton suggested a series of distinctions, not always to our minds very happily, between the French temperament and ours. The theme is fruitful and suggests a thousand variations. We wish to draw nearer to the French, and to do so we must find out what divides us from them. Perhaps none of the differences is in fact more far-reaching than this, that our neighbours know what they want, get it and enjoy it, while we ourselves are for ever seeking we know not what, missing what we might have, discontented with what we have. It is curious to consider further that each nation regards itself as idealist, and observes with regret the materialism of the other. To the English, the French are materialistic and sensual; to the French, the English are too materialistic to be sensual, they are gross, they are pitiable materialists. These misconceptions are in themselves interesting. The French nature appears sensual in our eyes because the conception of measure in enjoyment is foreign to us : *Tout bonheur que la main n'atteint pas n'est qu'un rêve* is a sentiment against which the English mind revolts, but which the French accepts as axiomatic.

> Man's reach must ever be beyond his grasp
> Or what 's heaven for ?

is the sentiment the Englishman responds to; the good the present day brings as little suffices him as its evil. To put it otherwise, the Frenchman, with his more passionate and more penetrative intellect, has discovered that the ideal is unattainable; he has emerged into a region of conscious disillusionment and become a practical man. The idealism of the Englishman is more intuitive ; and because he has not defined its objects, he has no means of discovering that they are not attained. He still reaches out for a beyond, and forgets, in so doing, the things by which he is surrounded ; with the result that so far as he suffers disillusionment, he suffers it unconsciously. He does not know what he wanted, he does not know what he has lost ; but he recognizes in a confused way that he can never have wanted what he has got. The best he can do is to put up with it. Resignation, beneath which hope still breathes, is his distinguishing trait. He manages to survive somehow in the midst of the muddle he has made, and dreams still of order and even of beauty. And he is not a hypocrite, though we can understand why he appears to be one.

In no aspect of English life does this confusion between the real and the ideal come out more disconcertingly than in the way we are housed. Miles, square miles, of 'tenements' or 'dwelling-houses' belong, of course, to our neglect, our grossness ; they represent, *in extenso*, the items entered in our industrial ledger for 'accommodation of labour'. The faraway object to be attained in this case was not heaven. But when this element is set aside and we consider what kind of home has been chosen by those whose position in the world has allowed them some margin for choice, we find that in the vast majority of cases their choice has fallen on the impossible, on some unrealizable ideal. Our thought turns, of course, primarily, to the London area, or County of London, as being that with which ourselves and our readers are most familiar ; and the most evident fact about virtually the whole of it is, that the people living there are wishing or half-wishing or making believe that they are living somewhere else. Consider the vast

spaces that lie between Clapham and Wimbledon and
will soon involve Surbiton in their easy sweep ; take
Balham and Tooting with their dependencies as far
as Sutton on one side and Croydon on the other;
can we imagine that the inhabitants of these wilder-
nesses are proud of their homes? If not, why are they
there? Nothing could be more doleful than to drive
out of London, no matter in what direction, and to
reflect—the very names of the houses impose the
reflection—that the whole portentous limbo has grown
up out of an instinct of escape. 'What is alcohol?'
a North-countryman was asked ; 'the quickest way
out of Manchester,' he replied ; and everywhere the
Englishman's first thought, where his towns are concerned, is the same—to get away from them. The
most depressing feature of the suburban pageant round
London is the exhibition it makes of the utter futility
of his tactics. One after another, down the interminable streets, 'The Elms', 'Bellevue', 'Oak Leigh',
with their privet hedge and their soot-grimed laurels,·
show us clearly that to the first occupiers the attrac-
tion of each locality and every villa was that it was
'in the country'. Here the poor ostrich, fleeing
before the invader, buried his unthinking head in the
sand ; and now the invasion has passed over him, and
all he can do is to keep it buried and to dream of the
oak or the elm or the *belle vue*, which survives only upon
his door-plate. Thus it has come about that nineteen-
twentieths of so-called Londoners are no true townsmen, and enjoy hardly any of the benefits of town life.
They are deluded hankerers after green fields. Each
of them craved for the beyond, and all have found
themselves outdistanced and buried irremediably.

This desire for the country is a touching instinct in
our people, but it has operated childishly. Having
refused to face the prospect of town life, we have no
towns ; we have merely conglomerations of drowned

suburbs. Civic architecture begins with the recognition that a town is civilization's crowning achievement. It is an achievement that involves certain sacrifices, including many of the delights of privacy and individual taste. Yet only in the town can human life fully declare itself ; here is the serious, the central work of man, here his most characteristic, his most essential enjoyments. This truth is hidden from us, where citizens are citizens against their will, where the first thought of each is escape and retirement, where the town is an accident instead of a creation. All English towns have, at best, this accidental quality. Or, if civic consciousness at last wakes up or stirs uneasily in sleep, its first impulsions probably increase the error. Our first thought is variety, and our town passes from unconscious into conscious chaos. Uniformity is, of course, the necessary framework for civic designing, and with it clarity and candour. But we must still be thinking of the country. A cant of nature worship has possessed us, and our idea of nature in a town is to make it seem other than it is : small if it is a large town, large if it is a small one. We have not at all grasped the fact that the honour and dignity of a town are self-contained, and that the nature it has to express is its own nature.

Yet, if we want to see the right ideas in operation, we have only to cross the Channel. What a humiliation it is for a member of the greatest seafaring nation of the world to embark at Southampton, with its incomparable harbourage, used merely, in that sense in which use means degradation ; its filthy sheds and wharves presenting everywhere their sides or backs to the quays, and behind them huts or lodging houses or some incredibly mean steeple ; and then, landing in a few hours at Havre, to observe that long façade of houses overlooking the water ! Who knows what goes on inside them ? On the ground floor, offices or

stores; above, flats, lodgings, tenements—they are
nevertheless of queenly beauty. They hold permanent
court, presiding over the loading and unloading of
merchandise, the arrival and departure of great ships.
They are the work of a nation that understands its
activities and the honour that is their due.

Mrs. Wharton's chief, or at any rate her justest,
claim for the French in the little book we have alluded
to, is that they are grown up. One of the most
valuable characteristics of the mature mind is its power
of surveillance, of keeping watch. More than all else,
it keeps watch over the element of desire, because it
recognizes that nothing but unhappiness can come of
desires to which the circumstances of life deny satisfaction. The French have applied this to the creation
of their towns. They do not romance about the
country, no doubt because their life is nearer to the
soil than ours is. They do not crave for the country,
for they are not separated from it. And then, they
are by nature better fitted than we are for the delights
of human intercourse. Therefore the mass of French
townsmen, whether they live in Paris or in the pro-
vinces, are happy to be in a town, and the more they
are in it the better they like it. We should be surprised
if it were otherwise. A French town is always noisy
and generally dirty; but how gay it is, how smiling!
The lofty house fronts, washed over with their pale
dim colours, breathe contentment and serenity; the
men who built so were glad to have neighbours and
wished to live in a close communion. A town was for
them the image of the virtue of associated effort, its
first beauty was its commodity, the subservience in it
of all that expresses individuals to all that expresses
and furthers their common ends. Hence the width
of the highways, the amplitude of the open spaces,
and the preponderance of rectilinear design. For the
straight line is the shortest distance between two

points, and the aim in the city is communication.
Hence, too, the predominance accorded to municipal
and public buildings, to the opera house, the theatre,
the picture gallery, the concert-room, all splendid both
in their fabric and in their framing. Add to this a
conscious love of beauty, a recognition of a common
element in man's work and nature's, and a desire to
relate them together. The works of man take precedence. His roads need not wriggle because rivers
do. His town must fulfil its human aim. And yet
a part of this aim is still to worship nature. Great
avenues line the principal streets ; the broad river is
not broad enough ; it is lined by avenues on either
bank. So conceived, so realized, the town is not only
a place of pleasures and a centre of affairs, it is a
mirror of the spirit and the mind of its citizens. It
is a lesson to the least of them of the dignity of man's
calling ; and the Frenchman who lives in a cellar or
a garret can still be proud of his home.

We are of those who hold that the future of civilization is threatened by diseases the poison of which is
town-bred, and to our sorrow and mortification we
are forced to recognize that this English race, whose
genius has more than any other to offer of solid sustainment and instinctive adaptability to the world,
suffers in its towns a grievous and a dangerous handicap.
Nor is there much consolation in reflecting that it is
partly through our virtues that we have fallen. There
is, of course, no excuse to offer for our wastes of slums.
But the hardly less depressing wastes of lower middle-
class suburbia derive, it would seem, on one side
from that peculiarly English faculty of expressing,
in the very stones of dwellings and not less in the
trees and garden plots grouped about them, a sense of
the beauty of the affections, and the worship of the
family as the setting in which these affections naturally
flower. In earlier days, when subtle and slowly

maturing perceptions had time to register and per-
petuate themselves in the daily handiwork of men,
this predominance of affection and intimacy, achieving
a mysterious compromise with the opposing requirements of town life, produced those miracles of way-
wardness, warmheartedness, and the heavenly pic-
turesque which we call Tewkesbury or Shaftesbury
or Burford. And at Winchester or Oxford—is it too
hard a thing to say?—it looks as though similar
affections, operating, alas ! in changing circumstances,
have produced at one time the sacred humanities of
the city and at another the interminable monotonies,
cruelties, and defacements of the suburban areas. It
is hard, and yet in a sense it is true, and, after all, it is
a palliation. The beauty of the old English town still
haunts us, and, rightly feeling that it was never an
intended beauty, we have continued to hope that our
surviving love of home will blossom into other immortal
accidents. But Sutton or Surbiton are the kind of
accident which arises when warmheartedness is served
by the railway and cheap bricks ; and to all who open
their eyes it is evident that the principles which
made England's beauty in the past no longer serve to
make her beautiful to-day.

Centre of a vast Empire, she has motives for the
expression of the spirit of her civilization in its fabric
which France lacks. In a different sense from
France, she has an appearance to keep up. ' This
precious stone set in the silver sea ' has an infinitely brighter place in the world than ever she
had in Shakespeare's day, and her responsibilities to
the future are immeasurably greater. The beauty of
England has been and remains still a tie binding to
us with passionate loyalty many an exiled heart ; but
now only too many of these exiles have seen the land
of their desire and have suffered a terrible, an ominous,
disillusion. Mr. J. E. C. Bodley, one time Secretary of

the Royal Commission on the Housing of the Working Classes, writes forcibly on this theme in the course of an essay which he appended to his recent volume on *The Romance of the Battle Line in France*. Here is his account of the impression left in the minds of certain ' athletic Anzacs ' quartered in a manor-house near Rugby :

> Eton and Harrow they had never heard of ; but Rugby, the birthplace of the greatest of games, to have seen it would console them for hardship and wounds. So a detachment was presented with railway tickets and it proceeded to Rugby. The pilgrimage was not a success. The approach to the once pretty little market town near England's centre, described in Moultrie's verses well known to Rugbeians, is now more repellent even than those with which our fair cities of Oxford, Cambridge, and Chester are disfigured. The brave Anzacs followed from the station a dismal street worthy of a mining town, so mean that the sunlight of a spring day only emphasized its dreariness. The courage which had shone immortal at Gallipoli was cowed by the sullen aspect of modern British architecture.

The example strikes by its simplicity. These Anzacs had not read Ruskin. They did not want carving and Gothic arches. The most elementary recognition of civic propriety, a little dignity, a little human happiness in the appearance of things—they would have asked no more ; but everything is repellent, dismal, dreary, sullen. Our Anzacs soon turn in to a public-house to ' get away from it '.

Our towns express us before the world, no less than our free institutions or our poetry express us. But the influence of our poetry is felt occasionally by the few, and the influence of our institutions, though permanent and universal, is elusive in its nature. Our towns are a concrete, a palpable, an insistent expression of what we are, of what we are content to appear, of what, unless we mend them, we are infallibly destined to become. They are our present disgrace, they may yet be our eventual doom. For out of them must proceed one-half at least of the British race of the future ; and in their meanness, their monotony, their monstrous expansion, they offer nothing for the perpetuation, for the development of an Imperial people. Because our national temperament is long-suffering, because we have a gift for resignation, let us not suppose that British humanity is proof against every strain. Out of Peckham, out of Kilburn, there can in the long run be born at the best a lifeless respectability, leavened here and there with the wild spirit of revolt ; at the worst, and constantly, a passion for relief and distraction, for the excitements which bring forgetfulness. Such are the inevitable reactions we have prepared for millions of our fellow countrymen ; and these millions have our country's future in their hands. What kind of democracy can we expect of them? What kind of politicians will those Englishmen become, to whom England shows a face so vacant and so repulsive as to drive them for refuge to seek the mercies of oblivion?

The matter is of urgency at the present time for two converging reasons. In the first place, the squalor of our condition has been the by-product of a period of industrial expansion, and in spite of the difficulties of the moment a similar period lies ahead of us. We have its dangers to face, we have also its wealth to administer. To those who say, as we are now doing, that the country needs an architecture, the reply is always ' It is an economic problem '. All problems are economic. The simple truth is, that we were submerged in all this dreariness and bathos at a time of intensive production, and that our houses were beautiful while we were relatively poor. If our towns now desecrate the soil which once they consecrated, it is not because we cannot afford what we once afforded (for a man's work is now a hundred times as productive as it was a century ago), but because we

have not faced new conditions which no longer favour
beauty, and because we do not yet care enough about
beauty to pay its price.   Beauty is not a luxury ; it
is one of the necessaries of life, and every square mile
of suburbia means so much depression and degenera-
tion in our human material.   And then, though the
public mind is waking to the evil and is aiming at
a remedy, this remedy has the appearance of an
aggravation of the disease.   The recent Housing Act
has imposed upon all centres of more than 25,000
inhabitants the duty of submitting a town-plan to
the Government before 1927, and that is excellent if,
in the interval, we can discover what a town should
be.   Meantime it is proposed to build a million houses
on some hundred thousand acres of land, and it is laid
down that in urban areas the number of new houses
per acre is not to exceed twelve.   Now, one-twelfth
of an acre seems at the first glance a piece of land
worth having ; but we find, after making allowance
for roads and other spaces, that it means practically
a plot of the size of a lawn-tennis court.   Who would
not be happy to live in a lawn-tennis court if he had
the open country on one side of him ?   Perhaps this is
what our lawgivers were imagining.   But the imagination is vain.   These plots are not to be on the border
of town and country ; there is no provision for that.
They are to reduplicate themselves interminably, eating
up counties whole.   Thus it is the apotheosis of
villadom which we are inaugurating ; it is the con-
secration of the sentimental, childish muddle we
described in our opening paragraphs ; it is the worship
of petty individualities on a gigantic scale and at an
enormous cost.   The inhabitant of the new Belleville
is doomed to the listless contemplation for ever of his
own and his neighbour's insignificance.   He is to have
neither the benefit of country nor of town.

If the climax of our industrial development had

come, perseverance in old errors would be regrettable, but it would be less acutely dangerous. In view of the future to which we actually look forward, it is necessary not only that we should amend, but that we should atone. And our chief need is protection against the abnormalities of a machine-made world. We have been asked to roof London with glass that aeroplanes may have an arrival and departure station, and to construct overhead roads and rails. But that is the straight way to sheer insanity. Far greater than in the past is our need not only of escape from our cities but of happiness and humanity within them; and the new machinery, which is capable of destroying us, does now at last, in its perfection and power, admit of a reconciliation with humanity. For surely we have turned the corner; we have seen the worst that industrialism can do. The era of slavery and of industrial darkness is behind us, and the English, who then led the world and suffered more than any other people, have now a fair prospect of leading again and leading to better ends. With the internal combustion engine, the evolution of machinery has passed from its reptile stage. There is a beauty of adaptability in our modern appliances that has the inspiration of music. Our equipment is now so fine that instead of depressing it is ready to reinforce our aspirations and to establish them more surely. *Sursum corda*; we may say, even, *sursum corpora*; the whole body of our existence is making ready to soar; wings are the symbol of the age we have to inaugurate.

Beauty beckons to us among the promises of the future; squalor and ugliness threaten to overwhelm us under the mistakes of the past. We need and must have beautiful cities; we must at the same time have done with the disfigurement and destruction of the rural belts surrounding them. Even our garden city movement, which is so admirable at once in intention and direction, has this element of confusion for the bulk of us, that we think only of the gardens and so slip back unconsciously into that horrid acquiescence in endless doll's house plots. We say garden city and forget that the garden, our garden, can be no part of any city. It seems as if wherever we go that vision of a pocket square of mown grass must inevitably pursue us. The town or city belongs to the commerce of men. Space is of supreme value in it and can only be accorded to public pleasure. Private grounds are out of court. The private garden is the beauty of the suburban fringe, the meaning of which, however, is all in its transitional quality, its power to reach a hand to the town on one side and to the country on the other. Shall we not then now at last distinguish? We worship the country; let us sprawl over it no more. For the sake of the country (and after all the country feeds us!), and still more for the sake of our towns themselves, let us develop them intensively. There is room in London to house four times the existing population, while arranging for open spaces ten times their present extent. Let us prescribe limits for our towns then; let us draw lines of circumference around them from this day. And as for our future industrial expansion, is it not the ideal that it should be rural? Modern transport and the electrical transmission of power make this feasible, and the human case for it is overwhelming. Better even than the garden city is the industrial village. For the factory worker with his eight leisure hours is lost in a town; he loves and seeks the excitement of the life, but his character is undermined by it. What he needs is the country, the true country where in his spare time he may become a producer of bacon, of the necessaries of life and its sanities, instead of a consumer of cheap luxuries and a disseminator of poison. Meantime our towns themselves must contract instead of expanding.

Instead of spreading they must rise. Not, indeed, we hope, to mountainous altitudes ; it would be sad if our flats should ever look down upon our churches ; that would be a new monstrosity, heralding a new gloom. But there is no greater beauty in a town than spaciousness with all the amenities it implies, and height, economizing space, brings beauty. Moreover, villas and cottages are uncombinable ; they merely continue. Our town populations must be housed in town houses : in buildings which, remaining duly subordinate to great public works, may yet constitute, in their disposition and their style, the adequate and reticent background for the ordered and open life of men in a community.

May 1920.

VIII

THE REVOLUTION IN THE MIND

MONTESQUIEU, before the Revolution in France, like Tocqueville after it, was a fervent admirer of English institutions. Sainte-Beuve even goes so far as to suggest, in one of his *Causeries*, that he was partly responsible for the great catastrophe. ' In painting the government of the English in such bright colours, when after all he had seen its dark places with his own eyes, he seems not to have asked himself what the effect of his picture would be in France. Though he continually extols moderation in government, he does not often enough remind himself that this moderation is a quality which you cannot transplant.' But it was not only, in Sainte-Beuve's eyes, the love of England which misled Montesquieu ; it was also a certain idealism, ' infiniment honorable ', but based on inexperience.

In spite of all Montesquieu felt and foresaw, one thing was needed to complete the education of his genius and bring his nature to its perfection : he needed to see a revolution. He did not believe that wholesale proscriptions and robberies were any more possible in our times. Speaking of those of the Romans, ' We draw this advantage,' he said, ' from the mediocrity of our fortunes, that they are less precarious ; our goods are not worth the trouble it would take to rob us of them.'

This easy confidence, Sainte-Beuve points out, was a grave defect in a great intellectual leader ; it is not more dangerous nor more false, he says, to be a Machiavelli, believing that men will always do wrong when they can do so with impunity, than to be a Montesquieu, believing that they are naturally timorous and that their first need is peace.

N

The French Revolution came. It is still currently supposed to have been, with all its horrors and even to a certain extent because of them, a spiritual event and a reviving influence. The critic of our literature connects it with a new atmosphere typified in our poetry by the change from the manner of Dryden to the manner of Shelley. Wordsworth, the greatest of all our revolutionary poets, was in France at the very time when the vast upheaval was brewing, and breathed in there, in all its intoxication, the air of hope :

> Bliss was it in that dawn to be alive,
> But to be young was very heaven.

Yet, whatever the consequences of the Revolution may have been elsewhere, in France and in England they were deplorable. England had no need of the ideas which the revolutionaries had aimed at establishing, since, in so far as they had any political value, they were of English origin ; what she needed was a period of prosperity and confidence to assist her in realizing and applying them. The explosion in France, the excesses of the French doctrinaires, checked the rising tide of liberalism and seemed to justify the sternest reactions, the bitterest disillusionments. Wordsworth himself fell a victim, and has even been flouted as a turncoat. We blame him for the second delusion ; we do not always remember to blame him for the first. Like Montesquieu he needed, in his youth, the sight of a revolution. When the sight came, it was too much for him—for him, as for many others as well. It is painful to think that some of the blindest movements of oppression in our history, urban and rural alike, date from the nineteenth century. The strength behind the violence in France was the misery of the peasants ; yet we continued, with that lesson before our eyes, to dispossess our own, while the advent of steam and the development of factory life found us unprepared to think of our new class of operatives except as a material to be exploited and a danger to be suppressed. As to the results of the Revolution in France, they are perceptible to this day. French politics have not yet thrown off the revolutionary taint.

Happily for us, the genius of England is not revolutionary. At the close of the great war the outlook was black in our internal affairs. Fear of violence was in the air ; the habit of violence had been acquired ; violence was constantly written of, spoken of. But, though organizations of immense force existed, though provocations occurred, a peaceful solution was found for every dispute ; and there is more and more reason to believe that our development will continue unbroken in the still uncertain future. Nevertheless, the revolutionary spirit is abroad, and we can recognize it by the prevalence of strange hopes. Providence has been said to hide his smiles under a frowning exterior ; whatever demon it be that incites to revolution has the contrary habit : the smiles come first, the frowns and the thunder follow. It is, indeed, to one of our revolutionaries that we are indebted for the title motto of this essay, himself the mildest, most confiding, if also most argumentative, of men : consumed merely, as we ought all to be, by anxiety for the good of his class and of all classes, for the good of the whole world. A railwayman, he looks back to the days when he and his friends were to have joined the miners as the *moment manqué*. ' Ah ! the strike was not the only possibility ; the strike was only the beginning ; there was the Revolution.' And, feeling now that the more perfect, the easier, instalment of the millennium has been missed by an inadvertence, he still toys with the dream-word ; for ' there is also ', he told us, ' the revolution in the mind '.

The meaning of the phrase was obscure, but it has

remained with us and appealed to us as a phrase
which deserves a meaning and to which we should like
to attach a meaning if we could. For how easily talk
of a ' revolution in the mind ' might, unless one were
careful, degenerate into cant, as talk of a ' change of
heart ' has already done. We have done nothing to
satisfy these great needs when we have given them
a name. The suggestion in this case seemed to be that
there was an alternative before us : a revolution of
some kind was inevitable ; it must be either internal
or external ; the external revolution was in abeyance ;
then might not the internal one at any rate be tried?
It sounds so simple ! You have only to suppose that
men's minds are subverted or revolved at will, that
they take off or put on their ideas as they do their
clothes and, at the expense of a mere decision, can
turn them inside out. We know, indeed, that it is
precisely the minds which reach decisions most easily
that are readiest to abandon them ; we know also that
to swing to this side or to that is to be biased. Clearly
the attitude of mind we require is one which involves
revolution in another sense : an attitude to which the
object is central, with the mind for its circumference,
the mind having so travelled as to have seen the
object from every point of view and to have recognized and reconciled the opposing influences which in
their balance and convergence are truth and life.
It seemed to us that the circumstances of our time
were, after all, favourable to the attainment of a mental
revolution such as this, and so we were led to reflect
upon some of the limitations and conditions set to the
revolving mind.

   Man is generally reputed to have the power of
detaching himself from his surroundings and proposing
to himself the problem of his response to them. If
so, the tragedy of his life is that he exercises the power
so little, that he so easily relapses into a creature of

mere custom, controlled in his action by the obvious, the predictable, appeal. We see in many parts of the world races of men who are as closely committed to their peculiar manners and constitution as the thrush to make its nest with mud or the finch with hair. We read of civilizations that have attained to equipoise and held a balance of vice and virtue and an even contest with nature through thousands of years. Nature herself, if we look at the case more broadly (and is not man a part of Nature?), though it has been said of her that she groaneth and travaileth in the pain of her longing for perfection—Nature herself, in all the beauty and perfection to which she seems to have attained, unfolds before our eyes a picture of contentment in an infinitude of samenesses and repetitions. The philosopher once said that identities were inconceivable and all was individual ; and perhaps what he said was philosophically true. The million offspring of the herring are themselves unlike each other, but it looks as if Nature enjoyed their similarity more than their differences. The cuckoo said ' cuckoo ' in the days of the Romans and says it still, ten thousand times a day. It never has occurred to him, and never will, that his meaning has been expressed. Nature tolerates the perpetual rehearsal and every day gives him five hundred caterpillars that he may have strength to go on with it.

These being the very conditions of our life, we must not complain if much of our human existence is passed after their pattern. Change and novelty, to which the mind constantly aspires, occur only at the fringe of the great ocean, which out of its vast depths of tireless immobility sends an all but invisible feeler towards the shore. We are ourselves that feeler. Surrounded on all sides by a life that merely repeats itself, sustained by these repetitions, partaking of them, how can we but cherish the quality which

distinguishes us from the mass? Man has but one
way of progress. Since he has to divert the course
of Nature, he must vividly retain the sense of his
distinction from her; he must develop to the full
the principle of consciousness in action which is his
birthright. That is one reason why he is suspicious
of mere habit, regarding it as a reinvasion by the
enemy of territory won from her; and that is why
from time to time he tolerates and appears even to
delight in the subversion of his own handiwork, of
achievements which it may have cost him centuries
to build up. He is apt to destroy what he has created
as soon as it appears to him to have fallen back into
automatism; he trusts and cherishes those things
which assure him the possession of his directive consciousness and enhance its power.

The problem of the intellectual life seems thus to
lie in a reconciliation between the conscious wave-
fringe and the vast unconscious ocean on which it is
borne. We have to weigh our purposes, our will
to change, against the huge volume of Nature's inertia.
We have to graft our movement of renewal and our
forward reach upon an understanding of those change-
less, tranquil bases out of which alone aspiration can
pass into attainment, lured neither into immobility
with the mass behind us nor into the impetuous rush
which would cut us off from it to disappear in sand.
How rarely, indeed, is our consciousness operative or
dominant! We are conscious at every moment of the
day, but the times when we bring some grain of
direction to bear upon the slow bias of events are very
few; and, while one detail absorbs us, the thousand
others on which our lives depend pursue automatically
their reckless course. If we cease to think, if we lose
the faculty of change, we lose our manhood; if, on
the other hand, we allow our thought to soar or
wander, if we forget the limitations of its power, the

very instrument of our salvation isolates and destroys us. We need to be continually incited to think, to be continually reminded how little our thought avails.

It is interesting to consider our position in the world to-day with reference to these fundamental requirements. The period before the war was one in which already, at least so far as our Western civilization is concerned, the problem for the human race was one of mental adaptation. Within that narrow fringe of change which is our life material conditions had, in our own memory, suffered a transformation so striking that we might have supposed ourselves inhabitants of a new planet. To face an enlarged and complicated existence there was only the same old humanity ; and its response before so many evidences of its shrewdness was a sentiment of pride and satisfaction. The majority of men felt sure that the mind which had produced the locomotive and the aeroplane would quickly learn their uses, and that the way was broad before us towards prosperity and peace. It might have been said of us, as of Montesquieu, that we needed to see a revolution, for our optimism was unschooled ; but revolutions are not all of the same kind, and the truth was that we had seen one but without seeing what it meant. The war came, and made universally manifest to the proud inventor of machinery that he was as little the master of his fate as he had ever been.

There is not a man now in Europe who has not, in successive waves of deepening disillusion, felt the menace of death fall upon the whole fabric of relations which is life in his eyes : the occupations, enjoyments, affections, devotions, purposes, the whole colour and flavour of the human commerce known to him, all, all at hazard. We knew it in England with the first sight of our troops on the march and when the first artillery trains rolled by. Instead of the security in which we had been rooted and to which we were inured, complete insecurity not only for our own country but for the world. How often has the experience been repeated since that time ! Again and again we have known the nameless shudder which reminds us that all we seem to mean in the present and to care for in the future rests on a hypothesis, and that our first concern for the world must be not that it may be bettered, but that it may survive. The advent of peace has not re-established us. We have still before our eyes enduring examples of political and social ruin on the widest scale ; we have become familiar in our own country with the appeal to subversive principles and methods, with the threat of action of that kind which, once started, can be neither guided nor checked and ends only in exhaustion.

It is far from our thought to rehearse griefs or to argue irreparable losses. With the little that is left to us of the world which we once knew there is yet, it would seem, some comfort to be drawn from the shattering crises of experience to which we are still so frequently subjected. Our state might be compared to that of a convalescent after a dangerous illness which has left him crippled. Handicapped in a hundred ways, he may yet find that the race is not to the swift, and that the gift of detachment and comprehension with which he has been endowed more than compensates for the loss of obvious aptitudes :

> Around the vase of life at your slow pace
> He has not crept, but turned it with his hands,
> And all its sides already understands.

The meaning of human existence has been intensified and thrown into relief for us by a new vision of it from below ; it is the old tale of πάθει μάθος, experience out of suffering; only, because all has been imperilled, all is in a new sense known.

Conscious of weakness, appalled by the immensity of our task, we often cry out that our need is of a leader. But that again is an instinctive rather than a reflective appeal. We have seen the world's great hope wrecked by a man who tried to lead the world to its realization. The tyrant presents himself to-day as punctually as ever when order cannot be maintained without him. A Lenin or a Trotsky can conduct the affairs of a continent ; but by an unenviable dispensation, which would not be appreciably bettered if they were greater men than they are. It was possible in the past for the mind of one man to form a mould into which generations of his fellows should unconsciously be fitted ; and the mould was durable according to the measure of his insight into the human psychology of his era and the material conditions of its environment. Our material conditions are now such that unconscious reaction to them is, in itself, a danger to the race. No disposition of life into which the majority of men were merely directed could any more be stable ; the very elements of a solution of our difficulties would be wanting in such a case. Our need is for a new understanding of problems which are new ; and these problems are created in the main by a continual widening of the sphere of normal human responsibility and initiative. Liberty is abroad everywhere, not only as an idea but as a circumstance. The cinema, the motor-cycle, the telephone, journalism are overflowing with it. Men can no longer be safely repressed, nor is it even wise to think very much of guiding them. They can only be guided by being taught to guide themselves. Once and for all, if we are to be saved, we must look for our security in its final stronghold, the universal individual mind. Progress may or may not be the general order of things ; human civilization has in any case burst certain cerements and emerged, curious and quivering, it knows

not into what world ; or say, if you will, that some
ironic deity has picked up the new-born imago and
tossed it into a strange element to see if it will sink
or swim.

Because of this strangeness in our condition, the
woful predictions of certain philosophers amongst us,
their comparisons of our Empire or our degeneracy
with those of the Romans, do not seriously strike
home. We feel on the one hand that nothing worse
can happen to us than has happened already ; on the
other that our circumstances, whatever their menace,
are too rich in possibilities, too full of the enticement
of the rapturous element of the untried, to warrant
tones of mere foreboding. We are playing for an
enormous venture, and the fearful upheavals which we
have witnessed still have at least this value, that they
are producing among us on a wide scale the very
commodity of which we have greatest need—instructed
minds. The revolution which machinery brought into
the world passed over us ; it was accompanied by
no corresponding mental revolution. Now, largely
through a wide dislocation between our consciousness
and its surroundings, we are aware on all sides of
the flash and detonation of these vast currents of force
which we have generated and which we have not
learned to control. And so, if our position is full of
danger, the danger is lessened by our growing recognition of it. For the sustainment and development of
modern life we need, not as once in tens or even
hundreds, we need in their thousands, men capable
of conscious participation in the whole human adventure ; and are there not indications already that we
are beginning to get them? Is it not a marvel after
all, when one reflects upon it, that our workers,
conscious of their strength and of their virtue, should
have resisted as they have the temptation to enthrone
their virtue by their strength? It is in the nature of

every class to believe itself the guardian of good government and the repository of worth. Even kings, in their once solitary eminence, could think of themselves in that light. Yet ' Labour ' has already shown the grace of an uncertainty ; and to what shall we attribute this grace if not to the stimulus and example, the liberal yet inescapable education, of passing events ?

We live in an epoch of transition. The world is new, and we have only one way to meet it : we must become new men. We must enlarge and intensify our consciousness to embrace unaccustomed distances and to retain in the rush of things its promptitude and its composure. How hard, how racking, these adaptations are ! That was an error of the poet when he compared the mind's swiftness with the swiftness of the tempest or the light. It is true enough that, sitting in my chair, I can think about Australia in a flash, but a six weeks' voyage separates me from it physically, and mentally the gap is not of weeks but years. If I am in Australia in six years, I shall not be in Japan in less than sixty. The glance of the mind may be swift, but it is also futile ; in power of fundamental assimilation and understanding our thought is slower than we can believe. Through the network of mechanical relations that we have contrived men appear together and act under a show of contemporaneity, when the real distance between them is of years and generations ; and even this is but one item in the new burden of our fate. Is it depressing or is it exhilarating to take up the morning paper, to see exposed there in a hundred columns a single day's events and to reflect that, in the day before us, our life is, in various degrees of subtlety, conditioned by every one of these events, so that to live it adequately we should need to be acquainted with them all? If we are to attain the enhanced receptivity which is required of us, the depression we too often now experience must pass into exhilaration and the sense of mastery.

We are still far from any such apotheosis. Yet in the mere fact of our depression we are perhaps exhibiting pains which may turn out to be the pains of growth. We have at any rate been saved from the fatuities of ingenuous assurance. We have passed through periods of unbounded hope, and have seen our hopes dismembered. We know what it is to feel the very existence of our world at stake ; we know even that it is at stake at this moment. Can it then be impossible for us to apprehend that it is at stake always, saved and made only by a persistent and increasing effort, in which we must have our personal share ? Let us once and for all acknowledge that life is overwhelmingly difficult, let us allow that most of its evils come of mistakes which we should make ourselves if we were in their makers' shoes, let us confess that we are every day making equivalent mistakes in our own position, whatever it may be, and we have touched the elements of salvation ; for us the ' revolution in the mind ' will have at least begun. For the future of mankind is indeed uncertain : we are confronted with barriers the mind has never crossed or attempted to cross. If we are to cross them, it can only be by a development of the sense of concerted responsibility on the very widest scale.

Man tends, we saw, to run into blind alleys, to imprison himself in them and stagnate. The restlessness he then develops finds relief at last in violent disruption of the walls confining him. He wrecks his life for a dream, and starts out a pioneer from its ruins. That is a terrible and a sublime necessity when men are indeed prisoners. They are not prisoners now. They are prisoned only in their own inadequacy, their sense of littleness before the vast horizons opening out on every side, the incredible novelties of power, influence, action, by which the routine of their existence is rebuked. In the humiliation and embarrassment of such a condition they may be tempted to run amok, to reply to the great challenge presented to them, the demand for creation and expansion, by nervous, childish impulses of impatience and destruction. The ' revolutionary ' spirit has no other meaning in our time. It is possible that the test may be too severe, that circumstances require more of us than we can compass, that our nature is inherently incapable of growing to the stature of the world we have made, or that its growth will be too slow to save us ; but the conditions of growth are there. Before us lies a future rich with unparalleled incitements. To meet it we must ourselves be changed. However hard the lesson, it will not, if we fail, be because events have failed to do their part in teaching us.

June 1921.

IX

LORD GREY AND *THE PRELUDE*

EVERY one knows the delightful paper on Recreation which Lord Grey delivered a few years ago before the Harvard Union, and which has been published for English readers by Messrs. Constable. It has many passages of classic simplicity ; the relations of athletics, of sport, of literature to life are freshly touched. Humour and candour, innocence and wisdom, never flowed together in a more pellucid stream than they do in these confiding, kindly pages which show the English spirit at its purest and its best ; nor could anything be more appealing than the quiet security with which, in an essay that speaks only of pleasure, the true place of pleasure, the quality of true pleasure, are allowed to appear. Much is said about natural enjoyments, and the genius of the discourse lies in the assurance it leaves with us that these enjoyments have really been felt. The concluding thought is reserved for the pleasures which belong to ' a keen sense of the beauty of the world ' and the sustaining power of such pleasures.

I found it so during the war [Lord Grey said]. Our feelings were indeed roused by the heroism of our people, but they were also depressed by the suffering. . . . The thought of the suffering, the anxiety for the future, destroyed all pleasure. It came even between one's self and the page of the book one tried to read. In those dark days I found some support in the steady progress unchanged of the beauty of the seasons. Every year, as spring came back unfailing and unfaltering, the leaves came out with the same tender green, the birds sang, the flowers came up and opened. . . . It was like a great sanctuary into which we could go and find refuge for a time from even the greatest trouble of the world.

In reading this passage one thinks of Wordsworth's invocation of Nature as he nears his conclusion in *The Prelude* after emerging from the nightmare of the French Revolution ; the wonderful lines beginning

> Ye motions of delight, that haunt the sides
> Of the green hills ;

and ending

>   The morning shines,
> Nor heedeth Man's perverseness ; Spring returns,—
> I saw the Spring return, and could rejoice,
> In common with the children of her love, . . .
>   in Nature still
> Glorying, I found a counterpoise in her,
> Which, when the spirit of evil reached its height,
> Maintained for me a secret happiness.

Lord Grey is, of course, a Wordsworthian ; but we are not suggesting that when he spoke as he did he had Wordsworth's passage in his mind. If he had had it in mind, he would have quoted it. He is a Wordsworthian in a deeper sense. Wordsworth did not care very much about books ; that is to say, he cared for them as few of the rest of us know how to care—but there was something else which he cared about far more. It is the same with Lord Grey ; and Wordsworth's poetry remains for him a book among other books, a particularly valuable and suggestive book, however, because the lines of his experience have in important respects resembled Wordsworth's. Wordsworth is a peculiarly English product ; there is not one of our great men whom it would be more difficult to imagine in any other setting than his own. Lord Grey, in a different sphere and in a different, a sunnier, setting, is also typically English. It fell to him to represent his country in the most critical days which she has ever passed through ; and every Englishman acknowledges now with pride that a certain virtue of grace, which we love to associate with the name of

England, has never been felt and expressed more
faithfully than it was then by him, in all it holds of
resolution and of sanity and of smiling courage. To
say that these two men are peculiarly English is to
say that they are bound to us by many and close ties.
The occasion of Lord Grey's presidential address
before the English Association has led us to ask what
some of these may be.

The fact that a great statesman is regarded among
us as a source from which literary appreciation of
the best kind may be expected is of itself significant.
The times are not so tranquil as to make it a mere
sinecure to lead the Opposition, even among our
peaceful Lords. *The Prelude* is not the kind of composition to which a mind surfeited with affairs might
be expected to turn for refreshment. But when it
was known that Lord Grey was to speak on *The
Prelude* every one assumed that he would speak upon
it with that intimacy, that fullness of knowledge,
which it is refreshment to share ; and no one was
disappointed. The critic among us is ordinarily a
little too apt to forget that his true function is to share
pleasure ; and he has perhaps also allowed the
aesthetical preoccupations of the time to warp him.
Lord Grey did not speak of *The Prelude* as if he were
counsel attacking the prisoner who had written it
and demanding why he had not written it otherwise.
He simply accepted the work as a poet's account of
himself which he had enjoyed and could enjoy talking
over. There is much to be said for criticism of this
kind : for the recognition in literature of the substance as prior to the tissue, for the readiness to believe
that a poet's ' effects ' depend on our hearing what he
has to tell us, on our taking his work at its face value.
Our literature has been great because it has had substance, because it has had such things to tell us as it
concerned us all, as it concerned especially our statesmen, to know ; and with this goes one of the principal

achievements of our race, that there is real solidarity
between our poetry and our politics. The statesman
with us is the man who, knowing life, knows the poets
because they are part of it. We differ in this con-
siderably from our friends and neighbours over the
Channel. We do not say that their statesmen are not
well read ; they may be better read than ours ; but to
combine poetry and politics in France is to be versatile,
with us it is to be steady-going. Nor will it do to
combine them anyhow. It is common in France for
the man of letters to rise by the might of the pen to
influence in affairs ; it is less common with us. We
have seen fluent and incisive writers take a place in
the House of Commons, and we have seen them hold
it very temporarily. We recognize the practical life,
the sphere of government above all, to be the goal of
manhood ; and the test of aptitude is not brilliance
but fibre, spiritual integrity, the sound, the inclusive
mind. We all welcome Mr. Baldwin in his new position because, if his intellectual range is still unproved,
we know at least this of him—that his mind and heart
will work together. There can be no statesmanship,
as we conceive it, without that partnership, and
there can be no poetry either. That, no doubt, is
why it is never a surprise to us when our political
leaders come forward as literary interpreters. They
are workers in the same field as the poets ; they can
speak with native sympathy.

Wordsworth is a poet to whom the English statesman, and not least the English Liberal statesman,
naturally turns. *The Prelude*, as Lord Grey reminded
us with amusing references, is an autobiography which
has a heroine : her name is Liberty. Wordsworth
goes so far as to acknowledge an

> over-love
> Of freedom which encouraged me to turn
> From regulations even of my own
> As from restraints and bonds.

This, he says, was a kind of cowardice ; yet he believes that good may have come of it ; and he may be said to have referred the emergence of the poet in him to the fact that he never knew control. The experience is not one which we should imagine Lord Grey to have shared ; it indicates, we can believe, one of the minor differences between a poet and a statesman. Wordsworth's insistence on the point in his own case sometimes suggests that he did not fully distinguish the accidents from the essentials in praising freedom ; at any rate, the interest of his life is not the absence of restraints upon him, but the quality of the freedom into which his unimpeded spirit entered. It is in this that we find him vitally sympathetic to us. To Wordsworth freedom and nature may almost be said to have been interchangeable ideas. To walk in the meadows and to watch the clouds is or may be to be with nature, but only in a secondary sense. Nature is hidden in these things ; even to see beauty in them is not always to see nature. And the converse may be true. Wordsworth is never tired of apostrophizing natural beauty, yet it might be questioned whether he had a distinguishing eye. His taste in scenery may even have been bad. He is careful to tell us that the period in his early life in which he applied taste to scenery was a period of disintegration. Nature was to him mainly visible nature because the eye gives us our widest range of intercourse with the world ; but he saw in natural objects not their features, but their intention and expression ; and the quality to which he was attracted was the quality which made them susceptible of expression, a quality which runs through everything. The value of this thought for us is that, if we do not share his predilection for rocks or waterfalls or clouds or solitude among them, we are not necessarily alienated from him. He can show us very good reasons for loving these things. But such love is not an essential of salvation. The field and the mountain are types of influences with which we must reckon in one way or another because they are within us, because they are life for us as for all else. Wordsworth tells us that we shall reckon with them most effectually if we taste them pure.

The virtue of nature in Wordsworth's apprehension was the sense it inspired in him of creative power calling forth in man a creative response as he contemplated it and intensifying in him the spirit of understanding and action. This is nature and this is freedom too, and an instinct for the coalition is one of the most precious inheritances of our English race. Dim and unconscious in the mass of our people, it rises into light in a mind like Wordsworth's and assumes a halo of inspiration. His life's chief work was to trace the origin and the development in himself of this supreme intuition; he did it, but his manner of doing it is, again, alike in its strength and its weakness, English to the core. *The Prelude* was written while he was still young, at the very time when his creative faculty was at its height; but it has few familiar readers. Why? Because he wrote it without knowing what he wanted to write, began it for the sake of clearing his mind and relieving a temporary depression, and went on in a vein half of pride and half of apology, feigning to presume on the long-suffering interest of Coleridge, looking for a justification for his work, telling himself that so much introspection was only justified because he was laying the foundation for some more glorious endeavour, because out of it was to come the great Philosophic Poem which it was his vocation to write, never perceiving that the great Philosophic Poem was no other than *The Prelude* itself. *The Prelude* lay in manuscript till Wordsworth's death; he had forty years for completion and revision. It is impossible not to think that he made use of them; it is difficult to avoid thinking that he used them ill. However, we do not yet know what modifications he may have introduced into the original text; we only know that as finally given to the world *The Prelude* is inconsequent and incomplete.

This inconsequence, which affects the atmosphere of the poem quite as much as its substance, is, we must repeat, an English characteristic. *The Prelude* is stiffly encumbered with rind and wrappings, and even when we have pared these away we still have a fruit that must be eaten warily; there are flakes and fibres in its flesh. At the price of these we obtain essences which we should not otherwise obtain at all. Had Wordsworth deliberately addressed himself to the task of spiritual self-revelation, resolved to shape the intimacies of his experience into a universally intelligible whole, who can doubt that he would in the end have revealed far less to us than he has done now? The success of the venture depended on the uncertainty of the aim. Wordsworth decided what he would do as by degrees he found out what he was doing; and, working thus in the part unconsciousness which gives a hand to freedom, he draws the really telling lines infallibly when the time comes for drawing them. Not to quote the famous things which everybody knows, we find the essential theme of *The Prelude* realized in a hundred passages such as this:

> While on I walked, a comfort seemed to touch
> A heart that had not been disconsolate:
> Strength came where weakness was not known to be,
> At least not felt; and restoration came
> Like an intruder knocking at the door
> Of unacknowledged weariness.

What a model of expression is this for our latter-day introspectionists! And is their vision, which we will not compare for depth with Wordsworth's, often finer? One of the most astonishing experiences we get from

The Prelude connects itself with the frequent allusions in the style to the style of *Paradise Lost* : with such tricks as the double negative in ' melancholy not unnoticed ' or the transposition of phrases like ' the world was all before them '. It might have been supposed that Wordsworth's instinct, having regard to the difference between his theme and Milton's, would have been to avoid any possibility of comparison ; or did he see that, if only because the difference was so great, there was no danger? However it came about, the surprising thing is that a comparison establishes itself in the mind, and that, in page after page of marvellous achievement, *The Prelude* sustains it. Wordsworth is a poet who stumbles and falls ; Milton is not. But Wordsworth took the experiences of a Cumberland schoolboy and lifted them to heights which Milton scaled with demons and archangels. After all, *The Prelude* does not live in passages ; it lives in its large flights. When we have felt the sweep of these, and when, having risen with them, we reflect upon the delicacy and power of their impetus, we forget the bumps and the collapses, and can feel that the essentials of great poetry were with Wordsworth as with no other poet that we know.

Long before *The Prelude* was finished, Wordsworth must have known that he was engaged upon a unique spiritual biography ; but to the end he never really saw the implication of his theme, its augustness, its finality. Had he understood the task he had undertaken, he could not but have carried it through, at whatever cost of personal pain. Yet *The Prelude*, as we know it, takes faith in nature and in freedom up to the barrier where they are chiefly proved and there abruptly leaves them. How pitiful, how absurd ! If we are to understand and profit by the revelations of intimacy, momentous experiences must not be held back on the ground that they are too intimate to be

revealed. Immense as was the effect on Wordsworth
of the Revolution in France, that effect, even while
the events were before him, was not absorbing, for
he fell in love ; and great as was his sympathy with
the popular cause, it did not prevent him from loving
a Royalist. The fact that Wordsworth was a mystic
and that the general tenor of his expression is ideal
and mild has led many persons to consider him a
cold-blooded man. But love is in fact the most
mystical of the passions ; it is the very heart of mysti-
cism, and its influences were for Wordsworth capital
and crucial. He loved, as we know, twice before
his marriage. There was Annette Vallon, and there
was also that Lucy, who knew how to engage not only
all his tenderness and piety in affection, but all his
imagination, all his strength. Wordsworth assures us
in a familiar passage that his creative thought clothed
all inanimate things and endowing them with human
attributes gave them ' a moral life '. It is a rather
mysterious saying, and lends itself to fallacious and
fanciful ideas. If Wordsworth himself ever indulged
such ideas, the death of Lucy dissipated them :

> No motion has she now, no force ;
> She neither hears nor sees ;
> Rolled round in earth's diurnal course
> With rocks and stones and trees.

No other words in our language give us as these do
Love and Death confronted, in a bare apposition. Yet
The Prelude has no reference to Lucy, no reference
to the nexus of experiences which culminated in the
poet's marriage, experiences which must have been
in the main tragic and constituted, we can believe,
a principal ingredient in that dark cloud which it was
part of Wordsworth's purpose, in composing *The
Prelude*, to throw off. But that they were dark or
bright is irrelevant to us. Love as it first entered

Wordsworth's life worked, we know, convulsively ;
it lifted him afterwards only to lead to an annihilation ;
it left him at last in green meadows where there were
still waters. The course of the events does not greatly
concern us, though there is significance in their mere
course. It is open to us all to conjecture whether peace
and adoration, or a bereavement felt to be irremediable,
or the continuing torment of a love surmounting
differences would best have served the poet in the
man. What it lay with him to share with us and
what he has not shared is love the culminating experience of the life of nature, the relation of man to
woman shot through with all those hints and intima-
tions of transcendent glory which gleam for him in
inanimate things, in the very 'rocks and stones and
trees' themselves, Love and Life in apposition. In
a passage of concealed yet touching beauty he finds
for us the inner link of the natural and the spiritual
in maternal love :

> Blest the Babe . . . who sinks to sleep,
> Rocked on his Mother's breast ; who with his soul
> Drinks in the feelings of his Mother's eye ! . . .
> Along his infant veins are interfused
> The gravitation and the filial bond
> Of nature that connect him with the world.

His mother's love gives him native sympathy with
everything beautiful, her pity his true adjustment
to the shocks of the world ; and in his helplessness he
hangs upon her not otherwise than the mind of the
poet, of itself also helpless, hangs upon the one great
Mind whose agent it is. Wordsworth had not known
much of a mother's influence, but he touches the
essential. That he did not so touch and illuminate
the love of the sexes in his Philosophic Poem leaves in
it a strange, a damaging vacancy.

But in this silence of his, in the nobility of his loves,
in the fact that though noble he could have wished

them nobler, and in his ultimate preference for smooth conventionalities rather than disturbing truths, he is English still.   If we take to ourselves Wordsworth the poet of nature and freedom, we must not less take to ourselves Wordsworth the author of the Ecclesiastical Sonnets, Wordsworth the monumentally complacent, Wordsworth whose last forty years of life were steady progress from poetry into prose, and, alas, that Wordsworth also who, when shown a statue of Cupid and Psyche, was heard to mutter ' Devils ! '   ' Since when,' Hazlitt observes, ' my feelings have been much altered towards Mr. Wordsworth.'   We have not any right to alter ours ;   at least, there can be few of us who have as much right as we might like to have.   It would   seem   probable   that   Wordsworth   not   only sinned and suffered, but that he also failed, whether in thought or action we do not know.   He was a poet and his poetry was his idealism.   His life was from within ;   no one had ever seen more clearly the dangers of compliance :

> Of genius, power,
> Creation and divinity itself
> I have been speaking, for my theme has been
> What passed within me. Not of outward things
> Done visibly for other minds, words, signs,
> Symbols or actions, but of my own heart.

But he was English ; and the English mind, with its gift for reconciling all irreconcilables, would reconcile freedom and compliance too.   Indeed the reconciliation is inevitable.   For freedom is for the intelligent, and few can really walk alone.   The rest are like the cab-horse in Dickens that collapsed when it was taken out of the shafts.   We need reins and blinkers. For most of us life consists of the external, the things ' done   visibly   for   other   minds,   words,   signs,   and symbols ' ;   and, recognizing that it must be so, we form our code and abide by it.   We abide by it rather too closely. We make the demands of the code so pitiless that even a strong man like Wordsworth, when he has contravened it, trembles, and is led at last to consider what others think of him more than the truth and reality of the situation out of which all thought and action, if it is to be his, must flow. Something like this befell Wordsworth, to his undoing and to our incalculable loss, and it befell him because he was an Englishman.

June 1923.

X
POETRY AND THE INTUITION
OF IMMORTALITY

POETRY is part of a universal tendency to beauty—
a tendency in the humbler walks of creation almost
universally realized. Beauty is paramount in the
natural world; and man, as he contemplates it, experiences delight and aspiration. He feels that there
can be nothing better than to be beautiful and that
beauty is the seal of perfection; and he sees, in beauty
itself, a twofold meaning. The beauty of a butterfly
is a miracle for which nothing in the nature of a butterfly accounts; heaven's rainbow has descended upon
a trivial insect's wings. Its beauty is its aptitude, the
contentment of its being; it is also the reflection upon
the creature of the spirit of the created world. It
is completion in incompletion. The response to it of
the perceiving soul is desire as well as delight.

In poetry man seems to identify himself with the
power that has thus found its expression in the
hierarchy of created things. The impulse of this
creative power appears, again, to be twofold: towards
perfection at each stage of an ascent, and towards
that ascent itself. Poetry has the same twofold impulse. In the ideal poem there must be the perfect
fusion of form and substance which is sometimes
identified with beauty and is one aspect of the beautiful;
the ideal is, in this aspect, static. The ideal is dynamic
also, because, as the poet's grasp of things deepens and
widens, its expression in terms of beauty takes corresponding scope, increasing in dignity and splendour, or
in freshness and radiance. There is thus a hierarchy
of beauty in the works of man as in those of nature.

Also, in poetry as in nature, though with a difference, beauty descends upon the work. The poet in conscious communion may obtain what is given ceaselessly to unconscious nature ; his fragmentary creation may be clothed with the spirit of the whole.

It is sometimes argued that, because the spirit of the whole thus descends, the idea of a scale of value in beauty, the idea of the hierarchy, must be abandoned. Beauty, it is said, the touch of infinity upon finite things, equalizes all it touches. It is a quality, not a quantity ; it is unmeasurable. To possess it is to lose finitude and embrace the universal. A mystical, yet an elementary, fact is here pressed and perverted. Heat is not measurable by the quart or the yard ; but we distinguish differences of temperature and have found a scale of measurement for them. And, though no scale has been found or is likely to be found for the measurement of beauty, which is not only a quality but a complex of qualities, yet the distinction of more and less in beauty remains, and is of the first importance. For the infinite permeates all finite things ; yet they differ in degree of permeability, in the fullness of the reflection they give forth. A poem so disposes certain materials that they hold and mirror the eternal light ; and though that light is one, though none can say what materials, how ordered, will reflect it most abundantly, abundance of light is essentially the poet's aim.

The importance of recognizing this is that it may enable us to unify our ideas of beauty and immortality. The very life of poetry is the immanent infinite ; the poet is he who on the whole best perceives the nature of the world, looking upon the things of time and revealing forms that are eternal. Yet even the poet gives us little clear guidance as to the relation of these immanent or transcendent eternities to our future. And the reason perhaps lies in our inclination to commit, on a larger scale, that error of thinking which in aesthetics refuses beauty a scale of more and less. Mesmerized by the infinite quality in beauty, lost in mere contemplation, we forget that this infinitude, this form we worship, must have its finite substance. And so, contemplating the world and ourselves within it and worshipping the eternal verities, the forms of things, we forget to ask through what substance these forms are made manifest, in what substance they persist. In fact, we use the word eternal in two senses, which we treat as interchangeable, while yet we can only begin to forecast our future when we have discriminated between them. We call eternal, truths and qualities to which duration is irrelevant, things which are not affected by the passage of time ; and we speak of an eternal life, meaning a life which will continue endlessly.

This confusion is frequent in poetry and takes peculiarly subtle forms. Philosophy is largely responsible for it ; and where philosophers have led the way it is not surprising that poets, whose minds least of all study the abstract, should have followed. The Eternal, we are told, is one who is ' out of time ', an Absolute Being, and Eternity is in contrast with Time, as though there were two states, the temporal and the eternal, one of which superseded the other. Poetry, of course, reveals to us the timeless aspect of our nature, enables us to take delight in unchanging truths. It suggests to us that the formulas of life, the laws, the conditions, of life are spiritual, and conditions, laws, formulas are all timeless abstractions ; it brings ever to our minds and itself exemplifies that most wonderful of all laws, the law by which life manifests itself in terms of beauty, and beauty itself becomes thus one of those timeless conditions of existence. And then, having uplifted and having dazed us, it will have us believe that these timelessnesses are the enduring realities, the life of the world. In this sense Arnold defined immortality as to ' live in the eternal order which never dies ', deciding, in fact, that the belief in immortality turned upon the confusion between the timeless and the enduring, and was illusory. Let us ourselves at least refuse to be deluded any further. The timeless cannot endure ; and what is the spirit if not that enduring substance which by its enduring makes time possible? For us the question of immortality is simply the question whether this enduringness belongs to individual men and women ; and we are now asking if poetry supports the belief that it does so.

The aspect of poetry which we have considered, poetry seen as beauty proceeding from a responsive mind, suggests an answer. For beauty is happiness, it is complete delight, it satisfies us. The morning air, the robin's song, the panorama of the heavens, a flower or the petal of a flower, does not the soul answer to these things, do they not summon us, do they not promise fulfilment for the whole of the soul's demands? The beauty of the world brings rapture, and the rapture is a rapture of security. Witnessing sublime harmonies, the poet works without fear ; for to-morrow can but enlarge to-day's promises, and he is himself one with the power from which this plenitude of beauty is poured forth.

Is this, or is it not, the fundamental intuition? Reason cannot tell us. But though we cannot discuss, we can in a manner test our intuitions ; and that which is best sustained and which most permeates and unifies the life based upon it is likeliest to be an intuition of the truth. Man's destiny has always been one of the chief themes of poetry ; and there has thus always been a conflict in the poet's reflective development between the intuition of life and the spectacle of death. In the modern world this conflict has taken peculiar prominence. Let us examine a few modern poets and poetic tendencies and trace the meaning of their different attitudes to beauty and immortality.

Meredith's poetry affords an excellent starting-point, because it stands at the apex of a long process of refinement. Expounding a philosophy of man in nature, it gave fresh stimulus to a general tendency in modern thought, in accordance with which the spiritual is seen in the actual, in the present world, and the distinction between this and any after-life disappears. The good is that which is good now, not that which might be rewarded later, and its goodness and value are inherent in itself. Meredith hints from time to time that a life after death is possible, but the tenor of his work suggests no faith in such a life. What, then, of the fundamental tone of his poetry? It is both hard and tense. Exhorting men to remember that life is good to those who make it so and welcome its bracing lessons, he never quite seems to speak from the heart of life, because his work never quite loses the note of courage and optimism. Now both these qualities really imply adverse conditions ; they suggest a temperament steeled to face an uncongenial reality. The spirit of ' he that shall endure to the end shall be saved ' is quite different, because in that we feel at once the fundamental assurance. We may argue, if we will, that Meredith saw the face of reality to be hard and resolved to make the best of things. But that is to write him down a hypocrite ; for his attitude is one of unreserving praise. It is more reasonable to suppose that the tone of artifice pervades his elations because he is asking of his soul praise and fervour for an order of things which, as conceived by him, no soul could praise completely, in which no soul could find perfect satisfaction. Determination, resignation, would be the highest response of the soul to the world were Meredith's vision the true one. And such an attitude leaves the intuition of joy in beauty unex-

plained. The soul demands more, and believes that
more belongs to it, as Meredith himself now and then
allows. The *Hymn to Colour*, in which more than
in any other of his poems beauty stirs a distinctively
religious emotion, contains his nearest approach to
a declaration of faith in immortality.

Matthew Arnold's poetry has more in it than
Meredith's of the quality of vision, and speaks more
intimately from soul to soul. Surrendering the belief
in immortality, he took poetry, with its revelation of
timeless beauty, to console and sustain him. He is
peculiarly the poet of spiritual disillusionment, one
may even say of spiritual bitterness. He calls upon
men to make this fleeting life worthy of the eternal
verities and to live in the light of contemplation. The
power to do this, he tells them, is their only immortality,
and almost in an agony he sees that, driven by the swift
wheels of change, they rise but seldom to any consciousness of the things that endure. To know the
Eternal is to have peace, and peace, he thinks, is the
soul's chief desire, and it cannot attain peace. Therefore the leading note of his poetry is solitude, separa-
tion, poignancy. He proclaimed a source of satisfaction
and himself did not find satisfaction there. It is open
to us if we will to throw over assurance and the
intuition of beauty, and to say that the reason he was
unsatisfied is that the world has no satisfaction for the
human spirit. But it seems more reasonable to say
merely that he looked for satisfaction to the wrong
source. If, as we believe, there could be no satisfaction
for man were he a merely temporary spectator of
eternities, distracted by the perpetual claims of the
mechanism of his body, the yearning note in Arnold's
poetry and his sense of the pitilessness of life explain
themselves ; and his message becomes essentially this—
that the eternal, in the sense of the timeless, offered
at best as a consolation, does not console.

This result is the more instructive because Arnold never loses sight of the organic interrelation of life and poetry, and applies, *mutatis mutandis*, the same tests to both. He holds what seems to be the true view of beauty, that to see it rightly we must see it as a part of the life from which it springs. He perceives that the life is more than the raiment, the spirit more than its perceptions or its forms ; yet he ascribes immortality to the raiment and the form alone. From him we may pass to a vast tribe of poets for whom art is the rescue from life of its one element of true value, the distillation and conservation of the still ' timeless ' element of beauty. Beauty is for them involved in life, else distillation would be impracticable ; and faithfulness to life is recognized, therefore, as a more or less necessary foundation for .art. But they value life less than beauty, and believe that the first condition of poetry is faithfulness not to life but to itself. The enjoyment of beauty is among a few things that go to justify the drudgery of existence, its waste, its boredom. Disregarding as much as possible the thickness, the crude substance of life, they would have us recognize that life can be lifted above itself, can be transfigured by the poet's skill, and that the true dignity of man is to rise, some would say by discipline of sense, others by liberation, into this loftier kingdom where beauty is enthroned.

This tendency is prominent in a number of English poets, in Rossetti for example, and William Morris, in Swinburne and Mr. Yeats. But, broadly speaking and associated, as in English poets it is for the most part not associated, with all that can give it equipoise, it is the French as contrasted with the English attitude to poetry. The resulting attitude to the question of a future life is one of patient or impatient denial, of attempted or accomplished disillusion. The patience and the accomplishment are with the French ex-

ponents of the school. A poet like Auguste Angellier
is faithful to all that is best in French traditions when,
by slow schooling of his perception and mastering of
his craft, he learns to touch the visible bounds of
human destiny with tenderness and justice, drawing
artistic effect from the brevity of life, the vanity of
wishes, the doom of love. An exquisite achievement,
a 'classical' restraint are the qualities by which this
poetry subsists ; and are these qualities, treasurable
always, and essential here, essential to all poetry?
Is this the fundamental note? Beauty is the acknowledged aim, and is beauty a thing capable of being
handled, possessed, on terms like these? Is this the
same beauty as that which on a butterfly's wing wakes
wonder and desire? The English followers of the
school, in their very inadequacy, answer the question.
The element of intoxication in such poets as Swinburne
and Rossetti, fatal as it is to work aesthetically conceived,
brings them closer to the heart of poetry. Their
enthusiasm for beauty, in the mere fact of remaining
uncontrolled, suggests that they have seen qualities
which the French overlook. Something external to
themselves, entering into their work and distorting it,
while it lowers them as artists, lifts them as poets.
They possess, and the typical French poet lacks, the
element of adoration in their attitude to beauty.
Beauty does not leave them spectators ; and the confusion in their work is the result of a misinterpreta-
tion of the summons of beauty, that summons which,
we might almost say, French poetry learns to ignore.
For the accomplishment, the stillness, of French work
have a quality as of deep water, containing and covering an unacknowledged regret ; and its very beauty
springs from an inverted admission of the truth it
appears to deny.

The tone of adoration may be heard in the work of
many poets who have supposed themselves irreligious

or believed that the only gods of their worship were impersonal abstractions. But we do not look to poets for logical reasoning, and shall not be surprised if they never trouble to reflect that the emotion of adoration, which is love tinged with awe, has necessarily a personal reference. The delight and desire which are our natural response to beauty are, when that response is pure, a religious delight and a religious desire. And just as the sight of the eye implies colour and a visible object, so these emotions of the spirit imply the existence of a spiritual being as the object which has evoked them and towards whom they are directed. Love is more than beauty, and the quality we observe in created things of a beauty that has descended upon them is the gift of love. Beauty pointing us upwards to this halo of love satisfies the soul and assures it that the demands of love will be fulfilled. But we know that in the life which death closes they are unfulfilled.

Just as there are many poets whose disbelief does not discourage us, so there are others whose belief does not appreciably add to our security. The immortality of the soul was an unchallenged dogma for many centuries, and a poet's assertion of it may bear no relation at all to that personal vision of reality which is his poetical gift. Herrick and Herbert, as ministers of the Church, announce one creed and remain in their verse the one primarily a pagan, the other perhaps primarily a priest. Sometimes, again, immortality as an intuition, a personal interpretation of the world, may be advocated, and the result may be the same. In Browning, for example, the intuition, though it exists, seems smothered by the advocacy ; and it is impossible to avoid feeling that his temperamental buoyancy colours his beliefs. But there are poets—Wordsworth is the obvious example, though his great Ode has no immediate relevance—in whom the intuition of immortality is life and breath. And it is in regard to these above all that our strictly pertinent question arises. Is there in the best work of Wordsworth, or in the Lyrics of Blake, or in Traherne or in certain of Vaughan's poems (to name a few of the more obvious cases) a tone which has, as it were, caught the pitch of the creation's dominant note? Have we here the essence from which whatever in all poems is poetry derives? Is the world or is it not an object of adoration? Is he or is he not the poet who is lost in praise and wonder? Is art an ecstasy in the service of an achievement, or is it an achievement in the service of an ecstasy? Has connoisseurship or has worship the ring of truth? If worship—where is the poet who has serenely and steadfastly given praise to a world in which he has felt himself a transitory stranger? Such praise, because it is impersonal, is sometimes accounted the noblest, and it is not a final argument against it that it breaks down. It might well break down, even if it were based upon the truth. The argument against it is that the impulse of praise in us has another direction. The note we are tuned to, the note with which the spirit of poetry harmonizes, is the note of a devotion which gives and expects all.

September 1916.

XI

THE EVOLUTION OF WORLD PEACE

In a volume [1] which raises a host of interesting and some ultimate questions Mr. F. S. Marvin has organized an appeal to history for a verdict as to the goal of human evolution, calling to his aid a number of able writers and students, some conspicuous for their knowledge, others for their idealism, and all deeply concerned for the welfare of the League of Nations— our great contemporary adventure in the better organization of world politics. Evolution goes its own pace, a very slow one ; and though it is true that the hand of man is now on the steering-wheel, there is little reason to suppose that his foot is on the accelerator. *Festina lente* is a good motto in every department of affairs, and of all achievements deserving our pursuit peace is the last that can be taken with a run. The material conditions, the attitude of mind favourable to it, cannot be too frequently studied, and we can imagine nothing more helpful than the organization of conferences and symposia where persons of influence may make an exchange of views and, temporarily breathing an atmosphere saturated with this greatest of all projects, emerge to spread abroad a contagion of sanity and goodwill. So let us ourselves begin quite at the beginning and frankly ask, if peace is desirable, in what sense it really is to be desired.

We instinctively associate peace with perfection ; amid the cares and turmoil of this world we long for

---

[1] *The Evolution of World Peace.* Essays arranged and edited by F. S. Marvin ; the Unity Series, vol. iv. (Oxford University Press, London : Milford. 9s. 6d. net.)

the peace of heaven ; we believe of our dead that they are living, and our prayer for them is that they may ' rest in peace '. Yet we have no experience of a life that is not a balance of forces, that is not based on contention and antagonism, and we know of few joys comparable to that of the struggle against odds in which, while we struggle, we still hope for victory. Are there then to be no further victories for us? Must we remain for ever content with the limited achievement of our brief life here? It seems improbable ; and except to those whom the world has wearied and overborne, it must surely seem quite unattractive too. Indeed, to ask for peace in this sense is perhaps not very different from asking for extinction ; it is, as the poet reminds us, the counsel of despair :

> Sleepe after toyle, port after stormy seas,
> Ease after warre, death after life does greatly please.

If we remove from life all thought of the antagonist to be faced and vanquished, it has no further call to effort and there remains for our consolation nothing but a philosophical abstraction. Such, too often, is the heavenly peace to which we are asked to look forward ; and is not our conception of peace on earth cast frequently on the same mould? Is it not mainly a negative peace : absence of rivalries, effacement of differences, fusion of particularities and individualities in a vague general good? Peace more or less after that pattern has been attained over large portions of the earth's surface at various periods of history. They are not the periods to which we look for inspiration. Formative periods in the history of our race have, alas ! been associated with violence and bloodshed ; only too often in the past the leaders of civilization have taken one another by the throat as the nations of Europe still incline to do, while peace has dwelt among peoples who knew of nothing worth fighting for, like certain inhabitants of South America to-day. There is no danger of the general establishment of a peace of this kind, which, if established, would deprive human nature of its best features. But there is serious danger of our allowing the thought of it, like a phantom, to disturb our vision; there is serious danger that an unacknowledged love of emptiness may sap the constructive energy through which alone a victorious fullness of human life can be attained. For, peace being an ideal, it is much easier to see what is inconsistent with it than to see what it consists of, what its positive qualities are to be.

We can best illustrate our point by some observations on Mr. Wells's lecture, a lecture devoted to that favourite idea of his, a World-Utopia. He begins his essay by asking what is meant by a Utopia and defining it in a peculiar manner. He says that the Utopian is simply the practical man : in this sense, that, if a man is going to build a house, he first makes a sketch plan of the building, and, *a fortiori*, if we are going to remodel the world, we must have our plan, in other words, our Utopia, before us. Utopia, he goes on, once meant Nowhere, since Utopians, being critics of the existing state of things, did not wish to be offensive to their neighbours, but that is all changed, and now ' Utopia has to be getting to business in international affairs ; it has to take off its fancy dress and speak quite plainly '. The fallacy of this seems to lie in its failure to discriminate between life and its parts, in the belief that a kind of action which is applicable to certain parts of life is therefore applicable to life itself. No one can plan for the world's future because, as the future gradually turns into the present, we find ourselves completely occupied in filling it, in being and becoming, in responding to the unpredictable offers it holds out to us. We can plan our house because we know with exactitude how most of the materials necessary to its construction will behave. We cannot plan the future of human society, because the reality of that future is the life of the individuals who are to compose it, and the complexion and formation of their life are not in our control. In fact, the very essence of a Utopia is its freedom from practical considerations ; the Utopian asks ' What do I want ? ' not ' What can I have ? ' His appeal is to the love of perfection that is latent in us all, and he makes it by presenting to us a society in a state of bliss, not asking how we are to attain such bliss, but what our bliss would be if we could attain to it.

It is a distinction of the first importance for all well-wishers of the League of Nations, all who wish to think of it not as a mere dream but as a practical proposal. Unfortunately Mr. Wells aggravates a confusion which might else have passed as merely verbal by the recklessness of his comments on passing events. The politicians and statesmen of the world have all proved themselves ' entirely inadequate ' in his opinion. They have not known ' what to do with the world, because they had no World-Utopia ready for this crisis '. They are all people of short views, by which he means ' people imperfectly educated, so that they do not see life as a whole, nor the problems of life as related in any intelligible way to one another or to any general scheme '. How curious that Mr. Wells should have discovered in all ' the leading people of our times ' the very flaw which seems to us to invalidate his own position ! it encourages us to think that the mistake is on his side. For if we do care really about establishing a league for peace, what channel of action can we find ? There is but one instrument through which we can work, our statesmen ; and if it should be true that they are all ignorant of what a statesman should know, there would be no help for us anywhere and no hope at all for the League. It would be pure Utopia then with a vengeance. But, of course, it is not the statesman's office to work by a plan. The material in which he works being life, it would be fruitless for him to decide in advance to what forms he would have it grow. His task is to divine what the vital forces at any moment really are, to feel the prevailing impulse of the nation he has been called to lead, and to direct it in the successive steps of its development. Now the things that are effective in politics, the influences that tell, are often those of which we are least thinking; for the relation of our thought to our growth is a remote one. Therefore, though the true statesman strives for an ideal, he forms no detailed picture for its expression. That is the Utopian's task; to the statesman it would be merely hampering. Utopias are fabricated of mind-stuff, floating phantoms; but the question for the states- man is, which among all those hovering possibilities can be seized and vitalized. He judges of what can be made vital by what has been made vital already. He is preoccupied with the idea in its embodiment, with the processes by which through such embodiment as has been achieved, the nation, all nations, may be led on to freer, fuller being.

Where could we find a better example of the differ- ence between an idea that is still floating and an idea that has been fixed than in the various associations of the word peace? The thought of peace flows through the mind like water, clear and lucid—our ultimate blessing, the fulfilment of all desire; the very condi- tion of a Utopia is that contentions should have ceased. But peace in practice, the peace our politicians have to secure, the peace we are hoping to build up in the future but for which we search the past in vain—how difficult are its approaches, how elusive it is, how contradictory! Few civilized peoples have thought war good, all Christian peoples have acknowledged peace on earth as their ideal; but they have generally pursued peace with a sword, and, when they have attained to it, it has never meant more than the temporary prevalence of one indisputable power or a temporary balance between competitors. All tends to show that in the realm of conduct something in ourselves or our surroundings is rebellious to peace; why else should it be so pleasant to think of and so hard to obtain? The paradox does not belong to the past, and we do not need to cross the English or the Irish Channel to find examples of it. Those among ourselves who have been loudest in praise of peace and severest in denouncing militarism have openly advocated the employment of force where their own interests were concerned. The difficulty, after all, is not with our politicians, but with ourselves; and the root of it is that, like Mr. Wells, we confuse Utopia and politics. The dream of peace is deep in our hearts, and we have as it were the moral assurance of having voted for it; so we lay the blame on our politicians if there is still trouble in the world. But peace cannot be arranged in accordance with what we wish or decide; it depends upon the tenor of our actions. Have we found what the principles of our conduct must be if peace is to be secured, or are we daily and hourly making demands upon the world which are exclusive and must at last bring us into collision with other men? Do we tend, when the interest of our clan or of our class is at stake, to assume that justice is on our side and that we must establish it by force if necessary? More generally, when peace and justice are incompatible, which do we prefer, and why? These are only a few of the more obvious questions which arise when we begin to bring the idea of peace down out of the dream world, to distinguish the political from the Utopian peace. But by the time we have found candid answers for them, we shall have stopped thinking of peace as a thing evidently realizable and lost by the stupidity or hypocrisy of our leaders. We shall have found that there is no cleavage between us and them. We have put them where they are to deal with a situation which we are making for them.

The vision of a Utopia works upon us by translating ideas into desires; the art of politics is their translation into life, their incorporation in flesh and blood, in a living and durable constitution. The field of its action is confined, the materials limited. True love, Shelley has told us,

> in this differs from gold and clay
> That to divide is not to take away.

There are, indeed, spiritual delights which increase as they are shared. But the texture and foundation of human life is still of clay and gold, and we are perplexed and harassed by the question who shall have the gold and who the clay. Before peace can be assured to us, all must have learned to value good things in their order. If we have never asked ourselves what we would give up, if need be, if we are in favour of peace because life has furnished us very liberally, if we are not quarrelsome only because our energies have full scope, our peacefulness is not practical; we are denizens of an accidental Utopia and our day of reckoning is to come. Nothing is more dangerous to the universal peace we now desire than the presence among us of innocent persons who, having felt no limits, no constriction, are unaware of the real nature of the problem; and there are nations of them in the world to-day. Our difficulties here in England are more often of another kind. The limits are already pressing in upon us strictly. We have discovered that it is folly for one nation to fight another for material things, since mutual destruction only means that there is less for both. But the absurdity is chiefly apparent

to us because we can call the two sides by different
names. It is one of the advantages of what is called
'internationalism' that the truth is dropping its last
disguise. The development of the hope of peace
between nations has synchronized with an increasing
disposition to use force internally, for mere redistribu-
tion of the clay and the gold. This enables us
to see how the problem of peace passes finally into
the problem of existence. The 'living wage', the
'standard of life' are wrapped up in it, and we divine
that there can be no ultimate solution until the problem
of population itself is faced. Utopia is now far away.
The establishment of peace argues, we see, the willingness and capacity of those among whom it is to be
established to strike the balance truly between the good
things of the material and those of the spiritual life,
to sacrifice the material to the spiritual when circumstances require it, and to build up the spiritual through
the material in the pure love of truth and of mankind.
The attainment of peace is as hard as the attainment of
wisdom, and the task before us the creation of a wise
world.

If such is indeed our goal, how useless is it to be in
a hurry! There are still with us three hundred millions
of men whose faith promises them heaven if they die
fighting for it, and twice or thrice as many more who
have not heard of any League and could not hear of
one, for their minds would attach no meaning to the
name. Nine-tenths of the race, if not children in
tutelage, are not fit to be more and perhaps never can
be. How immense the task which devolves on the
independent tenth, and how sad to find that at present
they are much more combative than their primitive
brethren! It looks as if growth and development
were in themselves a menace, as if the wider our
contacts with the world, the more frequent were the
occasions for rivalry and misunderstanding, as if peace

must be increasingly difficult to attain as men's desires
and activities expanded. Certainly the new problems
created by the complexity of modern competition
cannot be overlooked, and no attitude is more likely
to lead us to a disaster than the ingenuous assumption
that we have outgrown barbarism.

We are still far from world-peace, therefore, and fear
will not get us there if love cannot. It is useless to
tell us that we shall perish unless we are converted ;
the orthodox have played with the fear of hell for
nineteen hundred years, and the result is inappreciable.
Fear is the wrong method, because, again, it is based
on emptiness, on negatives, on the notion that peace is
there when we cease merely to disturb it. That is the
policeman's notion, and the policeman is the officer
of an established order. Before we can appoint him
our order must be established. It has been generally
seen that the League of Nations could provide no
guarantee of peace unless it too had its police to control
offenders ; it has been less generally seen that before
a world-order could be infringed it must have come
into existence, that you can only protect what you
have made. And the thing to be made is other than
an accommodation between existing forces. We have
to establish universally a practical habit of mind for
which the relation of might and right among nations
will be the same as it is among the individuals that are
members of a nation to-day. Everybody knows now
that the strength of a nation is no guarantee of the
justice of its claims ; every one knows that national
action is subject to the moral law. But the idea of
' sovereignty ', the idea that each nation must be its
own judge, still holds because of the insuperable
difficulties of the task of bringing together this motley
host of dwarfs and giants, whose differences of size
are themselves, it may be, insignificant by the side of
their other differences of age and temperament, of

manners, and of circumstance. Part of the Englishman's heritage is the enjoyment of liberties attained through centuries of growth and dependent on an instinctive respect for certain moral principles which have gradually received recognized expression in our laws and customs. The nations of the world have to create for their general guidance and government a similar body of authoritative principle and procedure, to transcend the present crude and jarring system of watchful and balanced forces and to reconcile their competing claims in a common allegiance to the idea of liberty under the law. Such an allegiance involves for many a subversion of their existing mentality, and for all a long effort of constructive politics in circumstances new to human thought. Suppose that the germ of English liberty is seen in Magna Charta and that its full embodiment was reached when every adult citizen obtained the vote. The intervening period is not far from a millennium. Suppose that the Magna Charta of the League was the establishment of the Statute of the International Court of Justice in December 1920. Shall we not be optimistic if we assign to the complete enfranchisement of all nations in the polity and parliament of the world an earlier date than 3000? For the work of development and integration will be far more difficult for humanity at large than for one State. However distant the consummation, the method is sure. Right will grow as it is respected, and will be discovered as it is applied; the true reciprocity of nations, as of individuals, will be determined by concrete decisions given to meet concrete difficulties as they arise.

Universal peace involves a world-wide organization based on a code which the nations must create by usage and consent. That consent will only be won as it comes to be realized that national individuality is enhanced by mutual respect and that the common life of the race is enriched by national differences. If peace is to be truly desirable—this is our last contention—it must come before us in the richest colours, bringing with it the whole of earth's good things, it must be the crown and completion of our activities, a positive and additional creation. We find the shadow of a contrary heresy in certain recommendations of some of Mr. Marvin's helpers in regard to the teaching of history in schools. History, we know, has not infrequently been used as an instrument for the intensification of racial jealousies and antagonisms ; known facts have been consciously misrepresented for the better nourishment of national pride, the minds of children have been inflated with a lust of conquest or revenge ; all that is an abomination. Yet the conscious handling of history for any purpose, even what may seem to be the best, must be strongly deprecated. To children, and to almost all those to whom history is taught, its themes are those of a pageant or a fairy tale ; as such they can be used, no doubt, to point any moral a teacher may have in view. But the history ceases as soon as the moral comes in. The object of historical study, surely, is to enlarge experience. There is, in the last resort, no substitute for experience, and those alone can understand history who have understood life in its immediate dealings with them. But the next best thing to experience is imagination ; and if any truth at all is to reach young minds through history, the perspective through which events are viewed must be that which the imagination supplies. It is no doubt a danger to peace and a misfortune for the League of Nations that written history is so full of wars ; it is a dislocation of life to present it so. But in poetry and even in fiction the same dislocation is to be observed. Our attention is constantly directed to events which in the very fact that they are critical are unrepresentative. The discovery of the turnip,

one of Mr. Marvin's essayists contends, was really of
much greater importance to England than the fate
of Charles I, for without it we should have been starved
by Napoleon and defeated at Waterloo; but even
its association with the possibility of defeat in battle
is not enough to make the turnip vivid. History,
for all but the maturest, must continue to disregard
what is merely solid and sedate, and to tease us out
of ourselves if it be only with the vision of the unjust
punishment of an unjust king. Its appeal must be
to the peaks, the points in its vast panorama on which
light rests and from which it is reflected to us; and
these peaks are always personalities in their ardours
and vicissitudes, with, next to them, embracing them,
our country struggling for freedom or for existence or
for enlargement, facing in this way or in that its
difficult adventure in the unknown. The imagination
is avid for these things; it settles and fastens upon
them and will not be denied. Truth is a relation
between the mind and its object; to change the
emphasis would not be in the interests of truth. If
we serve up to youthful imagination some artificial
food, it will not be assimilated; we shall merely
provoke a revulsion of taste. The thought of peace
and of the pursuits of peace emerges on a secondary
plane, reached after longer and profounder study. It
is a thought to which we cannot attain by substituting
one point of view for another; it supervenes. And
in the same way we cannot reach peace in reality by
any mollification of our souls; we must fill the measure
of our personal and our national individuality and overflow it. The spirit of combativeness itself cannot be
gainsaid; we must find how to reconcile it with
national as we have reconciled it with individual
rivalries.

July 1921.

XII

INDUSTRY AND HUMANITY

No problem is of greater urgency to-day than the humanization of the conditions of life for the masses of the people. We see the social fabric shaken or shattered in one country after another, and from every side the warning reaches us that men are rising because they are not treated as men. Unless we can so organize society as to allow every member a conscious part in its activities, unless every worker can feel his task self-chosen and himself responsible, a human unit, not a cog on the driven wheel, our civilization itself, we are told, is doomed. The better life or better arrangement of life is sketched, as a rule, in terms of political idealism. Democracy as a form of government is losing credit, but the principles supposed to underlie it are taken as the standard of perfection in most of the schemes suggested for the control of industry. The individual worker is believed to have a right to control the conditions of his work, a right founded on his ideal equality with all other individuals. He is not to be counted upon, therefore, to support a system which uses without consulting him. We must reform our conceptions. We must recognize that the determining factor in industry is the human factor ; a man's work, however modest, being the expression of his personality, and therefore in its essence unpurchasable, we must arrange that this work be an offering he brings, not a tribute wrung out of him. He must be a citizen at the factory as well as at the polling booth.

Every one is agreed that machinery, in spite of all the advantages it has brought us, has greatly increased the difficulties of existence by its depressing effect on individual worth. Individual worth is the test of a civilization, and it is imperative that we should restore humanity to its position of true precedence. But how is it to be done? The common assumption is that popular control of business would humanize business ; and if we ask why, no answer seems forthcoming but that the multitude, being human, knows the needs of humanity. Yet the purpose of business is to supply those needs, and it directly and constantly faces the question : are they going to be supplied? Humanization, however urgent, is a supplementary issue ; and popular control would be anything but a humanizing influence if, as a result of it, the previous issue was not met.

Two books [1] bearing on this grave question have reached us together. Professor Ramsay Muir, whose clarity and cogency of style make everything he writes a pleasure to read, considers what attitude should be adopted by men whose watchword is Liberty, and formulates an industrial policy for a possible Liberal Party. His book is admirably dispassionate, zeal for an idea never being allowed to obscure or displace consideration of the facts which are the condition of realizing it. He suggests lines of development for our system as it is, emphasizes the ever-vital truth that institutions grow, and reminds us that the readier we are to encourage various experiments and to keep our eye on practical results, the likelier shall we be to solve our problems—all of which is excellent. The volume *Labour and Industry* is of a different kind, being the work of twelve authors of every shade of opinion. It consists of lectures delivered lately in the department

---

[1] *Liberalism and Industry.* By Ramsay Muir. (Constable. 7s. 6d. net.)

Labour and Industry : a Series of Lectures. (Manchester University Press. 12s. 6d. net.)

of Industrial Administration attached to the University of Manchester, some practical, some theoretical, some revolutionary. Its diversity of view has driven us back to a consideration of the elements of the case. What are the ultimate conditions of improvement? The point on which those idealists who have the ear of the people seem weakest is the one essential point of applicability in their proposals ; too many of them argue as if the desirable became possible automatically when a sufficient number of people began to desire it. Luckily for us, the genius of our people is a practical genius, and we do not doubt that when they have emerged from present distractions, the facts that control industry will again be generally recognized. But if we are practical, we are not content to be practical and nothing more. It is in our nature to inquire into the meaning of the facts which claim our submission ; we are practical and we are also mystical. Beneath the general ferment there is the search for a spiritual idea ; our attitude to our hardships will change in the measure in which we can cease to feel them imposed upon us arbitrarily and can place them in an intelligible relation to the human feelings they override.

Now there is a general movement in contemporary thought which is of a kind to throw the whole of the material struggle into a new light. We recognize, as never before, that the chief motive of life is a transmutation of non-human into human values. The division which religion once drew between the interests of this and of some other world has lost its severity of outline ; even the narrower teaching has changed its tone ; and in a little while those for whom this life preludes another will probably agree with those for whom it is our sole adventure in believing that we are bound to avail ourselves of its material opportunities. It is not long since the blessings of poverty were piously inculcated. Every one sees now that a certain

degree of material well-being is an indispensable basis
for mere morality, while civilized life rests upon that
minimum of prosperity which can assure to every one
of us at least a chance to be human. It is absurd to
suppose that we are on the earth in order to learn
to divorce ourselves from it. That is nothing but an
hysterical diversion of the obvious truth, that our
first ideas of self-realization are unlikely to be the best.
No : we are here to understand, to absorb the world, to
identify ourselves with it ; suffering in that identification assuredly, but with the suffering that assents, not
with the suffering that refuses ; overcoming, where
there is obstruction to overcome, by the discovery in
the adverse forces themselves of the strength needed
for the subduing of them.

Our moral fibre cannot but be strengthened and our
zest of life enhanced by such a conception of our place
in the world. The world appears thus as an invocation,
a challenge. It is, as it were, waiting to become one
with us ; and it is not merely by its beauty that it
summons us ; that appeal we easily appreciate—there
is a further, a closer, a more continuous call. All the
weight and bulk of things, of what we call matter,
with its immense passivity, its concealed or apparent
energies, are on our side. They are part of that vaster
body in whose womb our smaller body has matured ;
and as we distinguish ourselves from our hands and
feet and yet identify ourselves with them, so with those
huge limbs which we call earth and water : they are
alien and nevertheless are of our substance. The problem of life is so to infuse them with our humanity
that they may become its instruments, to be to the
world what the world has been to us. This conquest—
we ought rather to call it this release—of matter is
the romance of industry ; and from time to time, when
a great bridge is built, or a new fabric invented, or
when some drudgery of the ages is disposed of by new

application of mechanical power, the humblest labourer feels the significance of the event in a thrill of victory and sees in a flash his dignity and his emancipation.

What chiefly baffles us, perhaps, in our relationship with the material world is the concentration, the abbreviation, we have introduced into all our signs of contact with it. We forget our aims in the abundance of the means of fulfilling them ; and the processes of fulfilment have passed out of our hands, we deal only in results. It is easy, in the case of a beginner in music, to see the relation of his music to his notes ; but, when we are under the spell of a great performer, we forget that his commerce with music turns still on his ability to recognize certain simple signs and to connect them with certain simple sounds. Everything we do has in fact its elementary physical implications. The general who plans the disposition of forces in a battle sits at his ease and gives orders, while the soldiers who carry them out struggle with brute matter ; the difference between them, from our present standpoint, is that the soldier touches the material world at one point while the general touches it at a million. To-day we are all generals ; but we are like certain generals who were promoted during the war ; we have learned little or nothing of what a general should know. In the complexity of the instrumentation of our lives we have lost music, and the machinery which should serve human ends obscures them. Gradually, nevertheless, this complexity must evoke the intelligence needed for its control; and in the meantime, in the very fact that it defeats, it stimulates and spiritualizes us. It is because we recognize this that we more and more apply our faith—that power by which we touch the heights and breadths of things—to material issues. The identification is an old one :

Who sweeps a room as for Thy laws
Makes that and the action fine ;

but Herbert's expression is not completely happy, for it half allows the very opposition we wish to override. Sweeping is an insignificant and monotonous job, a fatigue which has to be accepted with practical cheerfulness. To lift its monotony by a semi-mystical interpretation is a risky expedient ; there is more hope —shall we say ?—in round corners or the invention of the suction cleaner. But monotony in work can never be wholly got rid of, and even the fact that it is done in the highest service does not make it fine. The physical world is tireless, relentless in its repetitions ; they are the elements of which our life is composed, and the chief fault of the organizations by which we seek to master them is an exaggeration of routine.

Nor is monotony the worst we have to contend with. We have to take our place in a world governed by alien laws, where what survives of beauty and happiness is obtained only at the cost of wholesale destruction. The spiritual life presupposes the satisfaction of our physical needs, and the activities to which those needs impel us are at variance with our ideal. The insect eats its mate, the fish its young ; and as consciousness develops, all it can do is to enlarge the affections and restrict the appetites. Out of the struggle has come a being capable of reflecting upon it, and his reaction is one of dislike. Very well ; but the facts will not yield before his distress. The conditions of his own life are unchanged ; he can only limit his cannibalism, he cannot abolish it. Here lies the fundamental dilemma of our relation to the physical : that we are forced to live simultaneously on two planes, on one of which we fight for that life which on the other we learn to diffuse and to surrender.

Love is the law of our life, the soul of our aspiration ; but love neither clothes nor feeds us. We might all be loving and all starve. Our love, to be effective, must subsume a whole series of antecedent energies each of which was evoked by some necessity of existence, each of which, since our necessities are what they always were, we still have to maintain. Here, again, the complexities of our civilization blind us : it is not only our purposes which they obscure, they lead us also to forget our necessities or to suppose that they can be automatically supplied. When in our dream we build up the noble city and establish human life on a foundation of peace, are we, on waking, careful to ask ourselves whether the houses had stairs, and whether there were drains in the streets? Are we not apt to suppose that the aspiration for peace is of itself so virtuous that it must bring peace as its reward? While that is our attitude, we shall never attain peace. We live in a world of which love is indeed the flower, but in a world which is shy of flowering. There is a sense, no doubt, in which love is natural—an over-flowing tenderness is among life's first gifts. But against this tenderness is thrown at once the necessity of sustaining life; and to sustain life without violating tenderness is not in nature. The conditions of existence preclude an easy harmony, nor is this primitive tender-ness the love we want. The love we want is love the conquest, the achievement; and its growth among men neither has nor could have any resemblance to the movement of a natural law. Water runs down-hill, but love runs uphill, and the hill is there and always will be there for love to climb. The effective love of man to man, of man for the world, must be perpetually maintained by him against an opposing medium, must be created out of conflicting elements.

Our argument seemed tending at first towards an identification of man and nature, and now it has driven a deep cleft between them. Perhaps the truth is that they are not simply related, are neither wholly the same nor wholly different from one another. The old doctrine of the mortification of the flesh carried antagonism too far ; it has its counterpoise in the contemporary idealism which cannot distinguish dreams from realities and expects to humanize us by the vote. The truth still holds that there is one law in our members (to take the word now in its widest sense) and another in our hearts and minds. But the problem set for our solution, the divine problem of our earthly sojourn, is not the forsaking of the first law for the second, but their reconcilement, the realization of the second through the first. We are not to prize the spiritual for its aloofness, but for the closeness of its grip, for the weight it can lift, the bulk it can transfuse and vivify. Our moral life, our civilization, our humanity is therefore an achievement which we have constantly to renew, and the bettering of our lot implies always the sustainment at least of such goodness as is already expressed in it. Day by day we begin at the beginning and remake the whole from the foundations up ; and if we bow our heads before a wave of ' humanitarianism ', we must not imagine that in so doing we are obedient to our higher nature. For the higher and lower are interdependent, and we can only rise if we maintain our base. Here lies the weakness of nine-tenths of the objections to our economic system, that they have not allowed for the materiality of the conditions with which an economic system is necessarily concerned. More than half of us live on the verge of necessity, and upon more than three-quarters the problems of shelter, food, and clothing constantly press. We are reminded without intermission that we are of one flesh with a world of strife, and in that strife we have to take our part whether we will or no. We can only master our necessities by accepting their spur. Here we are, in our millions, wanting and ever wanting good things the stock of which it rests with ourselves to maintain or to increase, doomed to turn and rend one another if it should fail.

Only by tireless energy and resource can we hold off
the eventual discord. That is the situation of which
the economic law takes cognizance; it represents our
reaction to the non-human elements to which we are
forcibly attached, by which we are driven, and which
it is the triumph of our humanity to subdue and to
transform. Therefore if we attack capitalism for its
inhumanity, we are guilty of a misplacement of our
moral teaching. For capitalism is of the stuff of which
morality is made; its workings are blind, they are
attended by injustice and oppression, but it is neither
moral nor immoral in itself.. It is the material world,
claiming and inciting our energies, and we become
moral in our response to it, if we play the game, if we
give grit for grit. Its enduring merit and solidity is
that it is built for our necessities out of the materials
they provide. It is relevant, it is real. It rewards
the winners, but its rewards are not adventitious, and
if they make some rich, they need not make others
poor. Essentially, the rewards are given by the
materials themselves, they are automatic. No one has
imposed or decreed them; they come to all who can
learn to deal with materials according to their law.

There is the law of appropriate quantities, for
instance. Two logs will not make a fire, and you may
spend an hour of toil with your bellows to keep them
burning; six burn by themselves, while you toast your
feet in front of them and read at leisure. In most
operations there is in the same way a line of natural
inertia which must be passed before the material will
respond, and thereafter the response comes in an
increasing ratio until we touch at last the limit of our
capacity for directing it. From the law of quantities
follows what we might call the law of postponement
or reserves. If we deal with our necessities as they
arise, they keep pace with us and overwhelm us. The
resistances we have to overcome are constant, but the

toll of energy they take varies according to our method in meeting them. The more we arrange, organize, and foresee, the larger the returns for strength expended. Our first thought, then, in any moment of respite, must be to put up a barrier against the invading elements, so that we may oppose them not by an immediate physical contact, but on a predetermined plan. These protective barriers, in the more complex conditions of the modern struggle, are still, by happy chance, called our investments; and Nature herself might seem to have foreseen our need of them and to have accorded to man the means of vanquishing her in making him the slowest of all creatures to mature. His defenceless children oblige him to think ahead. If tools are the most familiar symbol of capital in operation, all use of tools presupposes the inventive and applying mind; and man is in this sense a capitalist by nature that the mind only develops under protection. If he is to engage in the material struggle effectively, he must be withdrawn from it till he is in his prime; above all, till he has learned the use of that most powerful of levers, intellectual address. The attempt to identify the interests of manual and intellectual workers is fallacious, therefore. Brain-work implies leisure, and leisure implies a society so organized that the conditions of life may produce it automatically. The interests of the brain-workers are those of the leisured classes, and for them the final reward of capital —its ' unearned income '—is also its essential virtue.

If ' unearned incomes ' are to be justified, what, we shall be asked, becomes of our thesis that the antagonism of materials, the necessity of contending with them, makes us men? The objection is hasty, yet it touches a point to which the whole argument leads up. In our economics we have to consider the organization of prosperity in its widest sense, and to rely on whatever motive-power will keep the great mill of

human endeavour perpetually turning ; therefore they
are based on the physical needs of the individual and
his immediate relation to the physical world proceeding
from those needs. The question what use he makes
of his goods if he succeeds in accumulating a store of
them or finds a store ready accumulated for him is of
very great consequence, but the first interest for all
of us is that the accumulation should be made. The
acceptance of wealth and poverty is in fact a test of
sanity in economic thought. We may long for a society
in which material possessions are proportioned to
desert, or in which all men give their services and live
in equality, innocent of material cares. If these are
the true ends, we must strive to perfect ourselves and
our machinery for their realization ; but they cannot
be economically imposed. You cannot make a man
disinterested by order, and arrangements which will
only work when men are moral are obviously inapplicable in a world which exists to moralize them.

But now, if wealth is our general aim, it is because
commerce with the material world has limitless
possibilities, and because, when we are released from
its tyrannies, the time for our moulding, humanizing
action has begun. True enough, to be lifted out of
the sphere of the struggle is a moral ordeal which few
survive : ' How hardly shall they who have riches enter
into the Kingdom of Heaven ! ' Yet it in no way
follows that because a life presents temptations it
should be avoided, and we might even ask if a heaven
into which we entered easily would be worth entering
at all. If we accept poverty, our opportunities are all
but confined to the lesson of renunciation ; our
morality is passive. Wealth opens before us a vista of
creative moral action. For some the treadmill, for
some the ladder of life, we see in the material world
a means of ascent for all : it is there that men may rise
by it. So there dawns for us the conception of an

ultimate economy governing all our use of the material instrument ; instead of money we calculate in terms of the happiness into which money can be resolved ; and once perceived, this dedication of all blind forces, this humanization of the world, is an ideal to which we constantly relate our action.

More than at any previous epoch the prosperity of the people is now in their own hands. The destructions of war have thrown us nearer than we like to our necessities ; but we shall shortly master them again if once we understand where they have placed us and by what kind of action they must be met. Thereafter, we have the right to hope for a time of spiritual expansion and the gradual harnessing of our huge apparatus to humaner uses. But we must live in order to live well ; and those who attack the means of life, though their attack be delivered in the name of goodness, do nothing to bring the good life nearer to their friends or to mankind. The conception towards which we have to strive is one by which all human effort may be co-ordinated for the subduing of the material world. The more we can overcome the inertia of materials and command them instead of being commanded by them, the stronger grow the foundations on which we rise to our more human task—the elimination from human intercourse of the world's natural bias towards strife. Unhappily, this bias persists in ourselves because of our physical constitution. Power brings oppression, and all are selfish, whether they are rich or poor. But the real antagonist is blind force, whether its seat be within or without us. In our modern life the menace has been enormously augmented, because our machines, in their ungoverned impetus, have us in leading-strings, because our very existence is machine made. All that is most deformed and monstrous in the growth of our social organism comes of these vast concentrations of power and of the defects of our will and understanding in the disposal of them. Yet by their means we have advanced some steps towards a solution of our problem ; more of us know happiness, more of us know what it is to choose our life and to direct our action, than ever before ; and now a new advance is to be made. It will not help us to hurl one blind force against another ; our task is to infuse light and purpose through the incumbent suffocating mass. We shall move on according to the measure in which we can learn to face our problem unitedly, with mutual tolerance for human frailties, recognizing that our difficulties are in the nature of things and that our victory is our manhood.

April 1921.

XIII

SPIRITUAL DEMOCRACY

'THE strongest part of our religion to-day is its unconscious poetry,' wrote Matthew Arnold in a familiar essay. 'Our religion has materialized itself in the fact, and now the fact is failing it. But for poetry the idea is everything; the rest is a world of illusion, of divine illusion. Poetry attaches its emotion to the idea; the idea is the fact.'

The tide of events has long been adverse. Our consolation and sustainment in this adversity has been the belief that our lives had value as the embodiment of certain truths which, whether or no they won the victory, deserved to win it, so that it would be better to die than to betray them. We fought for an ideal of freedom and for a hope of peace; and our race, still slowly disengaging its bruised limbs from the ruins of war, finds, to its relief and joy, that peace and freedom have not deserted it. It seemed at first as if all who

> loved chivalrye,
> Trouthe and honour, fredom and curteisye,

must have died in their cause, so terrible was the sacrifice. But we know now that peace is still pursued and freedom practised among us; we have had happy assurance that these are not only vital, but dominant ideas.

We have no fear of being thought fantastic if we take the Irish Constitution, the Washington Conference as texts for a discourse on English poetry. Events like these are the very stuff of which our poetry is made, unless it be truer to say that they are made by our poetry. It might have been by accident that the race with the greatest poetical literature in the modern world was also the world's leader in constitutional government. The two gifts, as they have matured in the life and traditions of the Anglo-Saxon mind, are, in point of fact, complementary. The distinction between fact and idea employed by Arnold in the passage we have cited is not one which can be pressed. Poetry, for him, was ' a criticism of life '; for him and for us, life is an actualization of poetry. Indeed, poetry is the only art which can embrace man's life in its continuity and developing expression ; no other art finds in government a natural theme.

But Arnold was lifting poetry high even above government ; he was suggesting that, as the conscious-ness of men developed, it would turn out to be in its power and influence indistinguishable from religion itself, tending to become actually that ' justification of the ways of God ' to which it has so frequently aspired. In his writings on religious matters the burden of Matthew Arnold's message to his fellows was that they were blind and had given themselves over to be bound hand and foot, slaves to inessentials. He poured irony and scorn on the dissidences of dissent and failed to consider sufficiently that in religious matters, as in everything else, the ultimately essential thing is actuality, in this case actuality of faith. Keeping this actuality in view, it surely would not be untrue to say that the Anglo-Saxon race, with the instinct for government, with the instinct for poetry, has the instinct for religion also. We are not characterized perhaps by widespread felicity, certainly not by unanimity, in our views as to the divine governance of the world, but we realize with solemn conviction how supremely important for all of us it is that we should be loyal citizens of a heavenly kingdom. Religion for the English mind is not something to which it subscribes, but something to which it holds and by which it is prepared to take a practical stand ; and religious differences are accentuated among us because each is loth to exchange a felt reality for an uncertain dream. We are bigoted because we are faithful.

But, in spite of our sense of the supremacy of religion, we have allowed—and this was Arnold's suggestion—a distinguishing quality of religious truth to escape us. We have thought of it, all men have tended to think of it, as if it were primarily historical truth, forgetting that the whole of history is in the last resort inevitably fable, that all that we call truth of fact is qualified by its subjection to time. The past is past; exact knowledge of what it was is impossible to us; we cannot renew it in our experience. To know truth of history would be to know what actually happened at a particular time and on a particular occasion, and such are the delicacy of the real and the crudity of all our means of recording it that history remains for us matter of imagination and conjecture. Truth of religion, Arnold suggested, was independent of any particular event that might have happened at a particular time ; it was not historical, it was poetical truth, belonging, that is to say, equally to all times and all circumstances, and to be looked for in the whole course of events : primarily, therefore, in the only events of which we have immediate knowledge—the events of our own lives and our own day.

Two generations have passed since Arnold wrote, and there can be no doubt that our minds have moved in the direction he indicated ; they have moved perhaps more rapidly than he would have liked. In the churches there is a disposition to forget differences and harp on an ideal of unity ; and it is interesting to reflect that in a country like ours, where the essence of religion is its appeal to the conscience of the individual, unity of religious belief is only conceivable if all sects withdraw the dogmatical elements of their belief from rigorous interpretation. 'The letter killeth, the spirit giveth life,' we repeat on every side : and it is but another way of saying that the strength of our religion is its poetry. However, this same disposition among the churches proceeds in part from the fact that each individually feels its hold upon the life around it weakening. It is feared that the message of Christ to the world is losing ground, and that in the turmoil and glitter of modern life men are drifting into the wastes of materialism ; and so a distinction is attempted between essentials and inessentials of doctrine, and it is hoped to retrieve the position by a combined attack on the ranks of unbelief ; for, it is alleged, on all that is most vital Christian believers are agreed.

In so far as the incentive to unity lies in the recognition of a common foe, the case is less hopeful and the movement less significant. For the existence of such a foe is, in the main, imaginary. Heretofore the strength of religion among us has been closely associated with its narrowness ; it has been our habit to cling stiffly to a series of precise articles of faith, and we have been split up into small sects because every word and phrase of our expression and reception of the revealed truth appeared to be of ultimate importance. It was in vain Christ told us that the Sabbath was made for man ; we resolutely upheld that man was made for the Sabbath. In so far as that state of mind persists among us there can be no sacrifice of inessentials for the sake of unity ; for it recognizes no inessentials. But it is hardly now to be found anywhere where men's minds are active. The currents of living thought have abandoned it to backwaters ; the tides have receded and left it high and dry. Yet faithfulness still remains a dominant characteristic of the English religious attitude ; our first requirement of our religion is still that we should believe it ; and, judged before this faithfulness, the whole conception of dogma is found to be irrelevant to life. Modern religious belief amongst us tends more and more to follow an independent course, sacrificing the strength and support of conscious community to the demands of rectitude and to its sense of what is real, so that it can be truly said that there was never more Christianity outside the churches than there is to-day, and that the chief rival —we cannot say the enemy—of the Church's Christ is the Christ whom for one cause or another the Church excludes from her communion. Broadly speaking, this Christ is one about whose history we suspend judgement, but whose thought and example we wish to apprehend and re-embody in their lasting, their poetical, significance.

Government, poetry, religion, if these are indeed our gifts, we have been happily endowed ; and the more so that they appear not as a string of disjointed offerings which the fairies brought to the christening, but as different aspects of the same disposition, implying and sustaining one another. Are we then really a poetical people? To a disinterested observer, our manners, the appearances of our life, must seem, as nearly as may be, the denial of poetry. Poetry is inseparable from beauty, and beauty—to judge by our national activities in the mass—is surely the element in life of which we are least aware and which we are readiest to sacrifice to any other. The sordidness of our existence has touched the danger-point. Our scientists are daily warning us that it is unhealthy to live in the dark and our economists that we cannot afford to throw fuel into the air. If we emerge from our fog, it will not be because we cared to see the sky ; and, the kindly veil drawn back, it will still remain for us to discover in how many other respects the clothing of our lives is dull and degraded. We seem then to have little faculty of reading the message of the appearances of things. Parts of our beautiful country remain still undefiled, and we move daily from scenes as lovely to scenes as abominable as the earth can show without any vivid consciousness of the change and without much caring to inquire why the same race must call both its home. Yet if we have little learned to control the conditions of beauty as an aspect of the external world, the reason is not that we do not care about beauty, but that we have thought about it principally in another connexion while, in our dealings with the external world, we have thought principally about qualities with which its beauty has little to do.

Our chief interest in the external world has been connected with its permanence, its staying power ; we have not so much observed its features as measured its weight, its endurance and its energy ; our chief care in life has been to relate ourselves continuously with these continuing forces, to establish our existence, to see how the world works and to work with it. Then, in regard to our lives themselves, having long and faithfully devoted ourselves to their material furniture, we have been free to detach them, as it were, from the whole of this vast apparatus and to oppose them to it ; and it is in our lives so detached—not a practical, but an imaginative detachment—that we have found our principle of beauty. We have thought of ourselves as beings placed in certain circumstances to which they at the same time belonged and did not belong. The outward life, the life which those circumstances determine, we have dealt with practically, all the while reserving the sense of an inner virtue which was the inspiration of our response to circumstances and was superior to them. This inner virtue, this inward life has been for us the dwelling-place of the beautiful, the focus of desire and aspiration.

When we turn from the outward to the inward, we

necessarily bring to the contemplation of the inward the faculties which our practical activities have developed. The universe is all of a piece ; the distinctions we set up between this and that aspect of it are arbitrary and partial. Having in the outer world loved stability, energy, and order, we are prepared to recognize and to cultivate in ourselves the inward faculties corresponding to them. Our bent is still for the things that remain, survive, grow, and are at peace together, for a present that clothes itself with the past and consciously prepares for a widening future. Apply this disposition to the affairs of men in their communities, and you have the spirit of government. Those only can govern who conceive of the political problem in terms of the human material available for its solution ; who recognize that the possibilities of to-day are conditioned by the achievements of yesterday ; who can place themselves as it were on the curve of a nation's developing consciousness and find how to extend and produce it. Apply the same disposition in the creative sphere of art, and its product is inevitably poetry. We cannot conceive of poetry issuing from a world condemned to irredeemable ugliness nor suppose for a moment that the fogs and slums, the villas, the commercial wilderness which make up so great a part of the modern English scene, are a negligible influence. Our poetry, in the degree in which it is still ours, repudiates these things and in the last resort, unless we can change them, we shall lose touch with it. Nevertheless, poetry is an art to which these outward aspects are relatively immaterial ; more than any other it is concerned, as politics are concerned, with what we have called the curve of human development ; the beauty which is congenial to it is the beauty which belongs to things that endure and change because they endure, the beauty of life and growth, in other words, the beauty to which we have

learned specially to apply the terms moral and spiritual.
In fact poetry, alone among the arts, has, for its
fundamental theme, the graciousness of right living ;
we might borrow a phrase from Wordsworth and call
it the smile on the face of duty. The truths which
it is pre-eminently gifted to express are those by which
the course of human life is governed in successive
generations, the truths which in our failures we fall
short of and to which in our successes we approximate.
Having said so much, what need for us to connect the
instinct for poetry with the religious instinct ? We
might almost say, from this point of view, that
religion is poetry in action.

Statesmanship is human action on the widest scale ;
it is the application of religion to affairs, it is the
creation of the world which poetry reflects or antici-
pates.. A nation that has the instinct for order, freedom, and development does not necessarily control
all the conditions required for their realization.
Beauty is one of the conditions of such realization ;
we are losing that. Who has not sometimes found it
difficult, gazing about him with bleared eyes, to
believe that these heavy-featured determinists, silently
proceeding to their affairs in the gloom and darkness,
are a nation of living men ? How significant, then,
how salutary for us are the events which we are now
witnessing, giving back to us, as they do, the direct
vision of the source and strength of our national life !
We need not rehearse what is in the minds of all.
But this at least must be said : we have clearly perceived in the demeanour and in the speech of all
the public men concerned in them their consciousness
of the need and quality of the time. Their action has
not only been wise ; it has also been touched by
spiritual emotion ; it has been a sign that England lives, and that she can recognize the ordi-
nances and accept the occasions which are alike gifts

of God. These are not thoughts which bear to be stressed. The events were conducted without explicit reference to them; there must be no cant in our celebration of the events. But it would be wrong to leave them uncelebrated. And the thought we have found most appropriate to the moment is the thought of a new step towards the identification of religion and poetry. For our leaders acted with a sense of twofold responsibility, and approached their task with religious seriousness because they knew themselves to be instruments of an enlightened nation's will.

Now it is a leading aspect of the universal truth, which religion and poetry alike express, that it is independent not only of times and places, but of persons also: ' quod semper, quod ubique, *quod ab omnibus* '; it is in principle democratic. In all the past history of the world we see religion manipulated by a priesthood and the interpretations and observances proper to it imposed upon the mass of mankind. It has been of the essence of every cult to surround itself with mystery and demand of its initiates the surrender of their judgement, that *abêtissement* which the logical mind of Pascal does not shrink from admitting as an ideal. The suggestion is always of a veil behind which only the few learn to look and, having looked, call on the ignorant, the many, to save their souls by proxy, through the virtues of credulity and submission. The Gods once acted in a deeply incomprehensible manner and committed us all to consequences which only men possessed of traditional knowledge and transmitted power can avert or foresee : such is the burden of historical religion with its twofold tendency to exploit peculiar mysteries and consign the interpretation of them to peculiar people. And it is against these peculiarities that the religious instinct of the time increasingly rebels. We have perceived that mystery is about us everywhere, that life is a perpetual miracle, that what religion teaches as isolated and unparalleled is a consistent, an unceasing process, that the drama of redemption, the pilgrim's progress of the soul, is in daily enactment. Nothing, we conceive, is true of the past which is not equally true of the present, which may not, indeed, be truer of the present if we can lift our minds and pierce to the essence and virtue of the Divine reality, so as to make them effective instruments of grace.

Into our religious sense, as into so many other spheres of life, the ideals of humanism are, in fact, slowly penetrating. Truth is for all, and for each there is but one source of it; its perception is necessarily from within. Side by side then with our political democracy, and sustaining it, there has developed the conception of a spiritual democracy based on this personal aspect of the universality of religious truth. Some of our humanists are inclined to apply this universality too facilely, to argue that the mysteries of life can be immediately apprehended by all who ' become as little children '; and no doubt many of the barriers which we find between ourselves and the better understanding of the spiritual in all its manifestations are inessential, are of our own making. But to become as a little child is not an easy thing; to learn the combination of innocence with experience is perhaps the last conquest of the sage and the saint. It is not our suggestion that the spirit of poetry and of religion has been found to be simpler of apprehension or more readily attainable than was once supposed; but that the problem of its attainment, the nature of the end to be attained, are differently viewed. We no longer measure our spiritual result by the numbers who have found truth, but by the numbers who are seeking it; we no longer dream of enforcing religious conformity, but of evoking religious susceptibility; we no longer suppose that ultimate judgement is visited upon the soul according to what it has believed by hearsay ; its judgement, we feel, consists in being and seeing what it is, and its salvation merges in its general spiritual growth. Not that we forget that salvation begins and ends in love, but that the problem of love and the problem of life appear to us inseparable. Love is that which simplifies complexities, life is that which complicates simplicities ; each for its working requires the other for its material ; and the idea that we can sustain the masses of the people and save their souls in a loving ignorance of the world is vanishing from our society.

Such is the spiritual democracy of the present day. Its inspiration lies in a new approximation of religion to poetry and of both to conduct and affairs. It is not concerned to deny the past and is content to leave historical questions in abeyance. It feels that the wonder of the world passes its comprehension and that human experience is too limited to be secure in denying anything ; but, in so far as orthodox religion insists on unique implications of unique events, it feels such uniqueness to be their least probable, their least demonstrable, and their least significant feature. It wishes in all it approaches to penetrate to the relevant, the inherent, mystery and, relinquishing all the adventitious heightenings of the superstition and the symbol, to bring truth to the test of life : in one word, to apprehend it poetically. It recognizes, finally, that it has a harder task before it than any that could have been contemplated under the old régime : the one was the pouring of wine into a bottle ; the other is the cultivation and training of every unfruitful member until it ripens and bears grapes.

January 1922.

XIV

MEETING THE MEGATHERIUM

IT was suggested a little while ago, when the weather was rather hotter or colder than we liked or expected it to be, that the construction of a new harbour in the Gulf of Mexico had deflected the Gulf Stream and that the conditions of life in England had been changed for ever. There has been no confirmation of this rumour. Rain, frost, and sunshine continue to surprise us with new ' records ', but that is because we have only chronicled their performances for a very short time ; the seasons are what they were. Yet the idea of a great change supervening upon insignificant causes is an instructive one. The world's balance of power is in fact so exquisitely adjusted that a few spadefuls of sand thrown into the water in one hemisphere may ultimately cover half a continent in another hemisphere with fire or ice. The huge machine of life is working always at full pressure, but its course can be influenced by the weight of a hair.

The value of the analogy, or the application we intend for it, lies in the domain of thought and its relation to the stream of human progress. An imperceptible movement of the mind may alter, not our climate, but our destiny. It is tempting, on the one hand, to regard the life of men as determined by mere force of circumstance. Man, we may incline to think, is what the world has made him, and, when his time comes, will be destroyed by the world by which he has been made. His peculiar human motives, his tastes, his individuality, are, on this view, his temporary possessions only, something he rescues and detaches from the material nexus which enmeshes him ; they in no way affect the course of his development ; they merely enable him, a floating weed, to put out helpless flowers while he drifts to a bourne which he can neither choose nor escape nor foresee. There is a tendency, on the other hand, for the directors of men to speak and think as if human affairs were fully subject to human control ; as if the constituents of a reasonable life were always the same and always available ; as if the lesson of life had been learned by the wise and was only not applied because so many men were ignorant or stubborn or foolish. There have, indeed, been eras of history in which, the material life having been stabilized, the whole significance of human action has seemed to lie in the finer spiritual adjustments, so that man, as he steered his frail bark in some sheltered creek of the great ocean, could think of the waters beneath him and the rocks on either side almost as if they were objects of his own making. But neither of the attitudes we have indicated appears to be the true one ; and neither of them can give our thought the peculiar impetus which it needs if it is to confront modern problems. If one thing is certain about our present condition, it is that we are not now in a sheltered creek. The huge forces on which our life has always rested, even when we were unaware of them, are now announcing their presence by uneasy shiftings. They are manifestly carrying the whole race along with them, nobody knows whither. Needless to say, we are not alluding to the winds and tides or any merely natural agencies, though our ultimate dependence on these is perhaps more frequently brought home to us nowadays than formerly. We are alluding rather to the material forces of the world as available to man for his own uses. Like children who have been accustomed to play with the levers and buttons and switches of a dynamo, we have ended by discovering how to

connect the current and set the wheels revolving.
What are we going to do with them? What are they
going to do to us?

The problem which confronts humanity is that of
the adaptation of the old life to the new limbs. It is not
a problem without its analogies in history. The world
was at one time overrun by gigantic animals, all of
which gradually disappeared, exposed to attack and
decay by their unwieldiness. The lesson of the past is
that survival depends, among other things, on the
maintenance of a proportion between the bulk of
a creature and its brains. Great strength, feebly
directed, turns sooner or later upon itself and is its
own undoing. What reason have we to suppose that
the human brain, which has never yet solved the
problems of existence and only slowly and imperceptibly adapted itself through a succession of tragic
failures and collapses, will prove adequate to its new
burden? We have lately seen terrible catastrophes,
and know that they fell upon the world in part at
least through abuse of strength. What ground have
we for expecting that we shall avoid other and still
more terrible catastrophes as our strength continues
to develop? And, more particularly, what is the
right attitude to adopt towards the danger, and is there
anything that we can do to lessen it?

If the first characteristic of the age is its materiality,
the second surely is its mobility. Our difficulties
arise not merely from the cumbrousness of our plesio-
sauric life, but from the perpetual fluctuations of
environment to which we have to adapt ourselves.
We are like a leviathan that must ape Ariel, a behemoth
charioted upon the wind. Movement, if we consider
the course of evolution, has clearly been provocative
of intelligence. The plant, for lack of it, lives in a
condition of eternal sleep. But it is not the animals
that move most that are most thoughtful; how

little originality goes with the vivid and diversified life of migratory birds ! And of our own lives—do we not easily forget how mechanical they really are, to what an extent our actions are repetitive, how slow are the processes by which a suggestion from the world about us is accepted and incorporated in our system? Among the most dangerous fallacies of the time is the notion that a combination of the symbols we call words necessarily conveys its meaning to every mind to which the words are familiar, almost as if a sound were the same thing as an idea. The only way to understand an idea is to live through an experience ; and the process of living through an experience is for most of us an extremely slow one—so slow that the ideas which we most value are those which, like the idea of freedom, have been racially acquired. What is race, in the last analysis, but a substantiation of ideas, and why do we expect other races in whom ideas not ours are animate to accept our ideas on transfer and to apply our principles? The experience of all animals except man is ineffective, except under conditions of rigid limitation ; remove them, however little, from their sphere of knowledge, and they are totally at a loss. The strongest of all instincts is the maternal ; and yet a nestling is only known to its parents by its connexion with the nest, and if it falls to the ground it becomes unrecognizable to them. Men are much more the creatures of their environment than they commonly appear to be; because they can frame detached ideas they attribute to themselves a corresponding detachment, and this personal detachment is in the main illusory. It must not be supposed that because we are animals we have nothing to learn from the other half of the world's kingdom. The trees stay where they are ; the animal, though he moves, only moves significantly while his life retains a centre of repose. Like the tree, he grows into his

place ; and the difficulty of our life at present is that
so few of us feel or know our place, or have a place to
know. Our minds are assailed by cataracts of impressions, which have the excitement, the alternating
pleasure and discomfort, of dream-fantasies, and exercise little more of formative influence upon us than
dreams can do.

The turbulence of the time comes out most clearly
when we compare the conditions under which beauty
is followed and found with those which have prevailed
hitherto. When we read of the discovery of an
Egyptian tomb constructed thousands of years ago,
we confidently assume that every object preserved in
it will be beautiful, and we are seldom disappointed.
But are we as much surprised as we might be, and can
we explain to ourselves why we are so ready to associate
beauty with old things and ugliness with new ones?
There are, of course, many minor causes for the
association—the harmonizing hand of time, the rarity
of independent judgement, and so on. When all
allowances are made, the truth remains that beauty
is forsaking the works of men ; and we need to inquire
why. Consider, then, that if a man built a house only
so much as a hundred years ago, he was obliged to
build it from the materials that were at hand, and,
since his neighbours had always done the same, every
locality had its own architecture. The village was
a natural harmony ; the wood and the stone of the
district were repeated in its walls and roofs and
timbers ; and, the best way of using that wood and
stone once found, the ingenuity of men was released
for decorating them. The essentials of beauty were
assured in the homogeneity of house and landscape ;
and the mind, dwelling on familiar features, penetrating their very grain and substance, learned to exhibit
them for their own sake and to enjoy them simply
for what they were. The process was one of slow

saturation, traditional adaptation, instinctive response. But what happens to-day when a man thinks of building? Whether he wish to spare expense or to indulge in it, his embarrassment is the same; he can bring iron, tin, slates, tiles, bricks, marble, mahogany from the ends of the earth. What is nearest to him is seldom what is cheapest, never what is most costly, and so there is little likelihood of his employing it; and if he desire to build beautifully he is on the whole likelier to miss beauty than otherwise; for the worst offences against taste are those which are committed with the best intentions. Is it because we care less for beauty and seek it less than men did formerly? We do not think it is. But the beauty by which men were surrounded and with which they seemed to surround themselves in earlier days was a beauty to which they were related as a bird is to the beauty of its nest. It was inevitable, and the inevitable enters our consciousness but dimly. Nowhere has natural beauty been more defaced than here in England; but where is it more intimately loved? Separated from Nature, we long for reunion; but before we lost her we did not know there was anything to look for, and so there was nothing to be found. The beauty of man's handiwork in the past has been as much a process as a creation, and of all that part of it which was process he was virtually unaware. But now the processes mean ugliness; they clash with nature; and out of the conflict comes the possibility of a complete aesthetic consciousness and of a beauty felt and created in every part.

What applies to our disposition of the appearances of things applies equally to our commoner and more everyday relations with them. The conditions of life favoured beauty in the past because they favoured repose, because they sustained the mind and gave it a framework for formative contemplation. Men did not think about beauty very much ; they produced it without thinking ; it grew out of them. And similarly, though it has always been their way to quarrel violently among themselves for the possession of the world and its treasures, they have on the whole appeared as masters of that treasure when they got it. Looking back over history, we often see wealth abused by power ; we seldom see wealth and power dissipating themselves uncontrollably. The difficulty for our race has been the narrowness of its opportunities, not the superfluity of them. But all that is fast being changed. It is the feature of our age to have involved us in a vast apparatus which multiplies a hundred and a thousand fold our capacity to express ourselves in our surroundings, but leaves us, for the time at least, with nothing more rational to express than we had before. In the meanwhile, the forces we have called forth work ; the machinery is moving ; and if life does not come out of it, there must come death. For order is not produced automatically ; it is a progressive creation implying sustained energy of control. Where, then, are our new energies, where is our new insight, to come from? It is as if we were set to draw harmony from the great organ of the cathedral while we were still practising our five-finger exercises at home. Our actions have to follow principles of ever-widening determination ; we have to direct a multiplicity of unfamiliar details, knowing that every touch which does not create destroys. The idea that nine-tenths of our activities can be left to the dictation of the nature of things working for good has to be abandoned ; the nature of things (which, for our immediate purpose, means the web of mechanical agencies into which we have translated nature) is working for evil at present, and working very fast. How are we to catch up with it? To do so we must make an advance comparable almost to that which divides animals from plants, and establish our lives anew from their foundation. The difficulties, the dangers are tremendous ; so also is the incitement, the opportunity.

Obviously the response of mankind in general to the new conditions which have been set up will take the form of an instinctive reaction. For the masses the opportunities and deprivations to which science has exposed them must operate like fluctuations of food and climate in the evolution of animal life. All that conduces to their obvious and immediate satisfactions they will seize upon, from all that they associate with pain and discomfort they will shrink, submitting only to necessity. It was not the giraffe's intelligence that lengthened his legs and neck, it was his appetite for leaves. The future of men likewise will be principally determined by the adaptabilities still latent in their organism and the trend of their subconscious appetite. A question of profound significance, which we have nowhere seen discussed, is that of the probable relative adaptability of the different races of men to mechanical conditions. What will be the effect of complete industrialization on the immemorial civilization of China ? Are the Japanese better or worse qualified than we are to avail themselves of the advantages and to avoid the dangers of factories, cinemas, and motors ? In so far as these things mean slavery or tend towards a life regulated externally by fictions, the Anglo-Saxon race is easily outclassed. The perils of popular submissiveness have been clearly demonstrated to us in Europe recently ; but the Germans are mere tiros in obedience beside the huge populations of Asia, who even die when they are told. If machinery necessitates regimentation, therefore, as some believe— and no one knows—the ' yellow peril ' is another name for posterity ; the future is in the East. The hope for Western civilization is that individual development

under democracy, in spite of all its waste in rivalry
and blunders of initiative, may find means to establish and fulfil itself, drawing strength from the very
severity of the test, and so may gradually emerge
from ugliness and brutality into a living equilibrium,
unstable as the equilibrium of life must always be,
and yet so well equipped with balances and compensa-
tions that shocks will be absorbed and progress remain
at least a possibility.

The changes that have come about are mainly, of
course, changes in the furniture of our lives ; and it
is an inevitable consequence of this that we should
find ourselves specially concerned in questions of
property and enjoyment, the relation of the individual
to the world's goods. With larger fields of material
opportunity continually presenting themselves to us,
our possessive instinct expands ; the more we have,
the more we want ; and the wealth which might
mitigate the competitive struggle intensifies it. The
abuse of money, too, lends force to the ideas of those
who would deliver men from its temptations ; and
the contrasts of extreme poverty and riches which
modern conditions of life expose, if they produce envy
in the poor, produce in many of the rich a kind of
disgust and weariness, inclining them to feel that their
possessions are not worth holding, since human misery
is their price. In some countries life is a perpetual
fever, where getting and spending vie in speed with
the throbbing motor and every pleasure vibrates ;
others are plunged into chaos by desperate theorists
who, to avoid evils they know, have pledged all to
the unknown, with its infinite capacities for evil.
The chief need of the time is a new motive, a fresh
inspiration for all concerned in the production or
the administration of wealth. It is here that the
analogy of the spadeful of sand may help us. Nothing
that any of us, nothing that the best of us, can do

will amount to more than that little spadeful ; yet, if we place our inappreciable contribution where it is required, we may turn the balance for our kind between extinction and a new era of progress. There can be no progress for rational creatures without a governing idea ; but if a few see and apply such an idea they will create an infection which the many will feel and follow.

That being so, it is a pity that the real argument against Socialism and Communism is generally missed and an attempt made to stifle theory in a vapour of indignation. Where interests are shared, order prevails and an ideal is realized. Bees and ants live communistically ; why should not we ? Why cannot we share all things in common? For the simple reason that we see something better to do. We might be compelled to abjure property, and order of a kind might in the end result from the compulsion ; but it would be a less valuable order than the order at which we are now aiming. We are striving to found our civilization upon the free action of individual men, and to make its material equipment a secondary matter. To rearrange the material world violently, divorcing men from their possessions, though the love of men is often invoked as a motive for doing so, is in fact to make men subservient to materials. The Socialist's error is primarily mechanical or political ; he has an ideal with which all can sympathize, to which no Christian can refuse sympathy ; but he advocates for its realization a method by which the better ideal would be destroyed. There is nothing subversive about the notion that our possessions are our stewardship ; the worldliest of Roman poets expressed it in a line :

> Privatus illis census erat brevis,
> commune magnum.

It is and always must be the ideal of wealth that it

should be used in the public service. But the Socialist
fails to see that, in taking it away from us, he takes
away at the same time our devotion. For we can only
give what is ours.

In a peculiar sense the motto for our time is in the
words *devoted possession.* We must go out into the
world to possess it ; and just because of the dazzling
novelty and abundance of its riches, our worst enemy
is carelessness and waste, not so much the waste of
excess as the waste of ignorance and lassitude. It is
only too probable, indeed, that our whole national life
is rooted in extravagance, and that is a side of the matter
with which we should seriously occupy ourselves.
Almost all English people consider that the Americans
are nationally extravagant ; a prominent financier who
lately visited the United States expressed on his
return the conviction that its population, at their
present rate of expenditure, would exhaust the available
resources of the country in ten years ; and who has not
read wonder tales of the land in which every operative
drives to work in his own motor? But the late
American Ambassador, whose love of England no one
disputes, gives the future to his own country without
the slightest hesitation, dismissing the English on the
ground that they are spending their capital and that
it is their capital which is their power. It looks as if
the extravagances of a neighbour were always more
conspicuous than our own. Yet no one visiting France
returns with the idea that the French are more lavish
than we are. The impression we get is that they spend
less money than we do and, by spending it to better
purpose, secure a life which is in many respects more
significant than ours. Can we not arrive, then,
at some controlling idea of propriety or decency in
expenditure ; is there no means of discovering what
a man, as a man, is entitled to consume? What has
nature ultimately in store for us? Are we all one day

to drive our cars, or shall we all at last be living as the Chinese coolie lives, sustained on a dole of rice of which we scrupulously count the grains?

The difficulty of answering these questions is that they present us with a convergence of infinites. We know that English coal and American oil will one day be burnt out ; but we incline to think that before they are exhausted we shall have found substitutes for them ; Nature seems to offer us resources which are unfathomable. We are left, then, with the problem of what a man can properly use ; and that, again, depends on his capacities, and to his capacities we can set no term. It is a problem which demands the continual application of practical judgement, a kind of mystical sense of what is appropriate and right ; and, happily for us, these are the very faculties in which the English mind is strongest, when it is in clear possession of the main facts and broad relations on which a judgement should be formed. What we really need is to adopt towards the material abundance and provocativeness of our time a religious attitude : to apply our religion fervently to the irradiation and redemption of the blind forces which we control : to see to it that all the energies which we unloose shall have their significant, their spiritual direction. And we have specially to bear in mind two aspects of our possessorship. The first is that, for reasons we have set forth, the very multitude of our possessions or possibilities of possession makes real possession increasingly difficult. We must not confuse possession of things with the mere legal title to them. The legal title excludes others, it does not include us. That alone is really ours which we weave into the pattern of our personal life, and which through us is endowed with human value. The second is that, since the value of material things is always human and can only be measured in terms of consciousness, no use of property

can be right by which human ties are weakened or
violated. The most obvious form of material appropria-
tion is eating ; it is obviously indecent to feast while
others starve. But the same kind of indecency
attaches, in various degrees, to all kinds of luxury and
self-indulgence ; everything that has mass and no
meaning, all occupations which reduce themselves to
a blowing away of gas, commit us to a kind of con-
nivance in a theft. The great business of the world is
run for ends more serious, which it behoves us to understand. All unproductive spending, all spending that
lowers the general balance of human vitality and
enjoyment, is robbery of the till ; and, not out of set
purpose, not through any degeneracy, but simply
because of our distractions in the unfamiliar clatter
and bustle which surround us, this is become our chief
sin against the Holy Ghost.

A test of true relationship between the possessor
and the possession appears at last in the supervention
of beauty, of which happiness is one of the forms.
How far, in these days, are the works of man from
any emulation of Nature's inevitable loveliness ! We
are become instruments of deformity and outrage—
no people worse in this than the English—and we
acquiesce in our atrocities, as if it were ugliness that
were inevitable. Our works are ugly because we are
dealing with a world which we have only in small part
made our own : because we are handling as ours
elements and influences which are still immeasurably
alien from us and have touched only the fringe of our
consciousness. Since all, to be used, must be appro-
priated, let us address ourselves to the task. Above
all, let us not allow the welter of the world's abuses,
the huge scale of its confusion, to disarm us or drive
us into a quasi-philosophical retreat. There is no
conquest in mere abstinence ; nor do they contribute
to a victorious issue who gaze upon the turmoil in

disdain or pity and help themselves to its conveniences in ironical aloofness. The ultimate test of the time is necessarily a moral one. We must first make our own the uses of the motor-car, of ' wireless ', of every other feature of this miraculous modernity ; we must make them our own, we must become one with them, since only so can we understand and humanize, feeling the burdens as well as the delights. This done, we have still to recognize that knowledge and possession, however hard of attainment, will miss the crown of beauty unless we stand aside and use what we possess devotedly.

March 1923.